BULAWAYO BOY

BULAWAYO BOY

A Memoir

Frank Stock

Matador
Unit E2 Airfield Business Park,
Harrison Road, Market Harborough,
Leicestershire. LE16 7UL
Tel: 0116 2792299
Email: books@troubador.co.uk
Web: www.troubador.co.uk/matador
Twitter: @matadorbooks

ISBN 978 1805142 973

British Library Cataloguing in Publication Data.
A catalogue record for this book is available from the British Library.

Typeset in 11pt Minion Pro by Troubador Publishing Ltd, Leicester, UK

Matador is an imprint of Troubador Publishing Ltd

For my wife, my sons and my grandchildren

Chapter One

Myra had the best liver in Africa. I don't mean her personal liver, the one near her gallbladder, spleen and transverse colon. I mean the chicken liver she chopped and mixed with hard-boiled egg, to be heaped on top of cracker biscuits and devoured so voraciously at every bar mitzvah reception that there was little room left for lunch.

Or was it chopped herring? I think not, but if my memory has so deceived me that it was chopped herring and not chopped liver, then I am equally confident that Myra's chopped herring was the best herring in Africa.

At any rate, it was on a fresh and sunny morning during break time one day in the grounds of our junior school that her son David pushed me. Although his true forename was David, as far as Myra was concerned he had a double-barreled first name, which only she was entitled to use, namely 'Mine-David'. Similarly his brother Mervyn was 'Mine-Mervyn'; the 'mine' to emphasise that if you messed with Mine-David or Mine-Mervyn, you'd have Myra to contend with.

Well, Mine-David pushed me and in return, alighting instantly on the most hurtful and defamatory response my fertile imagination could muster, I insulted the quality of Myra's *gehakte* liver. Offended on her behalf and on behalf of her liver, he challenged me to a fight.

What caused him to push me in the first place, I cannot at this distant remove, say. It could be that in a delusional moment triggered by exposure to the African sun, I mocked the liver first and then he pushed me. Whichever it was, matters had got out of hand for there I was, faced with a challenge to a fight.

I admit that I didn't want to fight David Watkins. For that matter, I didn't want to fight anybody; either then or at any other time. As a pastime, it didn't attract me. It wasn't part of my DNA or culture. You can count the number of Jewish boxing champions on the fingers of one hand and even then, you need only one finger. Max Baer was a champion in the 1930s and he lived until he was a mere fifty. I suspect that his mother wrapped bagels with cream cheese for him to consume in the dressing room before each fight, which resulted in thickening of the arteries, which in turn led to his early demise.

In any event, I wasn't built for it. My child's weight card shows that when I was five weeks old, I weighed only 6 lbs 11 ozs which meant that at birth, I was barely 6 lbs and that ladles of Nestlé's milk and spoonfuls of glucose had had scant effect. By age nine, the time of the great hepatic episode, I had developed beyond 6 lbs 11 ozs, for sure, but in general I wasn't considered robust. I'd already suffered amoebic dysentery, my ribs showed, my appendix regularly rumbled and I was prone to something called acidosis, a condition, as the name suggests, of excess acid in the system.

Neither was it my fault that I wasn't a natural pugilist. I was, all in all, not athletic. That is not to say that I abjured all attempts at sport. Indeed, I remain proud to this day that I once arrived third at the finishing line of a 220 yards race, an achievement which I trumpeted to my parents and brother without confessing that there had been only three contestants. But, that memorable event apart, I wasn't a sporting success, a deficiency which plagued and embarrassed me for most of my life, as when I was unceremoniously sacked as goalkeeper from my barrister's chambers' five-a-side football team when we were four goals down after six minutes; or when I tore a muscle using a rowing machine – not by pulling the chain's handle but in reaching over to take hold of it.

So a fight with David W was out of the question.

Even more out of the question was fighting in the school grounds. The rules of the school forbade it. So it was that when a prefect, a strapping blond broad-shouldered lad aged twelve, who sported a crew cut, swaggered by and discovered that Watkins had pushed me and that I had insulted Myra's chopped liver, the most prized *gehakte* liver south of the Tropic of Capricorn, he, the prefect, in a time before mediation became fashionable, sternly invoked the rule by which one was required to settle the unsettleable with boxing gloves in the school hall; a rule exemplified by the school motto which, when translated from the ancient Greek, said: 'Quit Ye Like Men'.

I would, as a nine-year-old, have preferred a different motto, one with a less archaic meaning of the word 'quit'. But there we were. Or there was I. And apparently the manner in which males acquitted themselves when faced with disputes, whether about the British Empire or Myra's liver, was to exchange blows with fists made larger by hard gloves, until one of the contestants was beaten down or feigned convulsions.

In the prevailing circumstances, I had no choice but to pick up the gauntlet. I was surrounded by at least a dozen eagerly sadistic youthful colonials; and I was confronted by Watkins, his round face red with indignation, perspiration glistening from every pore, the culinary reputation of his lineage at stake and his meaty fists poised aloft with a singularity of purpose that was difficult to misinterpret. He was ready to smack my nose. It was reluctant to be smacked. So the interference of the prefect was a reprieve.

Running away was a tempting proposition but since it would have been witnessed by a sufficient number to render denial of cowardice impossible, it didn't seem an option then. Years later, on a cold summer's night in London when confronted by the certainty of a severe thrashing by a tall motorist whose driving skills I had loudly questioned but whose considerable height only became apparent when he unfurled himself from his Aston Martin, the wisdom that comes with maturity dictated that I run away.

But Bulawayo in 1955 was different. Things might, I thought, change before the appointed day. Not many things, granted, given that the appointed day was the next. But still. Watkins might die of liver or herring poisoning. There might be a pogrom forcing both the Watkins and Stock families to leave the country, although in the Rhodesia of the fifties, a pogrom wasn't likely. Those in whose hands lay the instruments of power and discrimination possessed a more readily identifiable target against whom to prevail with the added attraction that by picking on the blacks, instead of on the Jews, they wouldn't be accused of picking on a minority.

So I agreed and we were made to shake hands, a custom intended to denote no hard feelings, inapt in the circumstances since hard feelings were all that there were. Still, I had no difficulty shaking hands for my hands were shaking of their own accord outside the windows of Standard 3, the classroom presided over by Mrs Hayes.

To the classroom of Mrs Hayes, whose son John was a classmate, a boy with sand-coloured hair and spectacles, we returned, Watkins and I; the room in which Watkins (so ran the entirely false accusation) had once, after being refused permission to go to the toilet, relieved himself on the floor. The fact that the story was a figment of warped schoolboy imagination, following a water spillage, was irrelevant. It was, so we thought, a good story. Whilst he and I stood there staring at each other under a large marula tree that crisp sunny April morning in the grounds of Milton Junior School, I deemed it unwise to revive the pissing accusation. It seemed unnecessary fuel to add to an already raging fire.

I confess that I was disconcerted by the proportion of those offering Watkins support and advice; a proportion in the region of 100 %. It wasn't that Standard 3 was particularly devoted either to Watkins or to his mother or her liver or persuaded by the justice of the contending causes; they simply thought it more satisfying to back the winning horse and, since I was giving Watkins approximately thirty pounds and presented a personal history bereft of anything resembling courage, the consensus was that he would win, an astute assessment based on a significant preponderance of probabilities.

So it was that at five minutes past one that afternoon – school in the sub-tropics began at 7.40 a.m. and finished at five minutes past one – why five minutes past and not one sharp is a question I still struggle to answer – I left for home in my Milton Junior School uniform, which comprised a light blue shirt, khaki shorts held up by a grey belt with a silver-coloured snake-shaped buckle, grey calf-length socks, black shoes and my shoulders weighed down by a satchel and the worries of the world.

Chapter Two

Home then was in Fife Street, number forty-nine, a bungalow which is now, or until recently was, occupied as a home for abused wives. It lies four streets west and six streets east of Milton Junior School. The town was, and remains, set on a grid system. The streets running one way are numbered avenues and those running across them were named after the Pioneers or the odd English peer, thus: Rhodes, after the adventurer Cecil of that name, Fife (the Duke of), Grey (Earl Grey – the earl, not the tea), Abercorn (the Duke of), Wilson (Major Alan Wilson who led a famous patrol), Borrow (Captain Henry who was second in command to Major Wilson), Fort (there was a fort somewhere nearby), Jameson (Leander Starr, a mate of Cecil R and prime mover of the Raid which, no doubt to his chagrin, took his name), and Lobengula.

Spot the odd man out.

Lobengula was the son of Mzilikazi and the last king of the Ndebele who were an offshoot of the Zulu. Mzilikazi was a senior sidekick of the great Zulu chief Shaka but, having incurred Shaka's wrath, made haste with many followers in a north-westerly direction from Zululand to the area later known as the Transvaal where the voortrekkers held sway. As was his habit, Mzilikazi fell foul of them too and fled across the Limpopo to establish his kingdom in Mashonaland and Matabeleland some time before the British South Africa Company decided that it would like to live there too.

Lobengula's royal kraal was called Gubulawayo. The name was not original, for there was once a village of that name in Zululand.

Lobengula's prime connection with the Pioneers was that he had been persuaded by them, under the type of pressure to which Watkins was now subjecting me, to confer mining and land 'concessions' to a Mr Rudd (hence 'the Rudd Concession'), Mr Rhodes, Mr Beit and other members of the Pioneer Column which in about 1893 led to the plucking of another jewel for the Victorian Crown. With the plucking came bloodshed but, insofar as those of pale complexion were taught anything of the history of that part of the globe, the heroes were the Pioneers. Lobengula's kraal was razed to the ground and he fled north towards the Zambezi River and was never captured.

A word, in passing, about Captain Borrow: according to an entry in 'The Downfall of Lobengula' (Willis and Collingridge, Rhodesiana Reprint Library p. 242), a book not written from the perspective of the Ndebele, Captain Borrow had spent three years ostrich farming in the Cape Colony, harvesting feathers for his cap perhaps. The same work includes a contribution by one Major Forbes about the forceful occupation of Bulawayo and the part played therein by a certain Captain Bastard whose lifelong *sang froid* in the face of such a name can only be admired.

After the demise of colonial rule in the 1980s, the numbered streets remained numbered as before, but the names of the Pioneers and peers, except for that of Lord Fife, were expunged and replaced by names such as Jason Moyo Street, Samuel Paraneywata Road, and of course Robert Mugabe Way, though 'way' refers to the nature of the road and not to his political way which is altogether another matter. More recently, some of these replacement names were themselves replaced to cater for regional political preferences and to challenge those short on ink; so, for example, Vera Road has become Naison Khutshwekhaya Ndlovu Road and George Avenue is now supplanted by Emmerson Dambudzo Mnangagwa Avenue, after Mr Mugabe's successor as President. It is likely that at the very point in time when correspondents in that neck of the African woods become accustomed to penning the new names, further changes to the political landscape will dictate yet another substitution of addresses.

Then there was Main Street about which no political considerations arose so it was still permitted to be called Main Street for a while, but is now Joshua Nkomo Street, after the father of African nationalism in that country, himself an Ndebele, a tribal association which Mugabe found irksome. Main Street was notable for its post office, a sandstone building of considerable size, as well as for the Grand Hotel, purchased in the Watkins era by a man called Harry Shur.

Harry was a dealer in cattle hides; a person with no vestige of social graces, as shabbily dressed as a pauper but as rich as Croesus, who each morning distributed bags of three pence pieces – colloquially known as 'tickeys' – to African children in 'The Location', the part of town where most Africans dwelt. He bought the Grand Hotel in order to fire the manager who had had the effrontery to ask Harry and his dog to leave the dining room because Harry was feeding chicken bones to the hound under the table at which they – Harry and the dog – both ate. Why the manager objected to the dog crunching bones in the dining room of the Grand Hotel, neither Harry nor his dog could understand, so the dog stayed and the manager went. Harry Shur was a pioneer in his own manner but no street was named after him.

The streets are broad; the broadest town centre streets you ever did see. It was said that Cecil Rhodes had ordered the streets to be wide enough to permit a span of forty oxen to wheel freely from one street to the next. History doesn't relate whether this was ever put to the test or why the number forty. Be that as it may, the streets are wide enough for angular parking on each side as well as for a central parking reservation or divide. The town planners had catered for drainage by ensuring that at each intersection, the road dipped down and then up and then down again to enable torrents of rain water to sweep along the gulleys thus created. This provided excellent fun for young motorists who negotiated the tarmac roller coasters at high speed and for children who, after a rainstorm, waded barefoot in the newly formed rivers of light brown muddy water.

There was a statue of Cecil Rhodes in Main Street. It is no longer there. It has been replaced by a statue of Joshua Nkomo. Indeed, statues of Cecil Rhodes have been coming down apace in such other countries as once displayed them, in response to the colonial repression they are said to represent, though the benefit of Rhodes scholarships continues to be bestowed and accepted.

Bulawayo was built before the advent of the skyscraper, which is not to suggest that the coming of the high rise to the rest of the world made a jot of difference. It was a town of single-storey constructions, of bottle stores, pharmacies, Kingston's the book shop, Bata the shoe shop ('Buy Bata and have the shit kicked out of you' was the schoolboy joke of the time), Naakes the picture framer, Townsend and Butcher the sports outlet, Shappys the paint store (where lottery tickets were always on sale), the Standard Chartered Bank, the Palace Cinema, the Dairy Den drive-in ice cream parlour, the off-white City Hall – the perimeters of which were a hive of curio vendors displaying their wares on the sidewalks – and quiet department stores, such as Haddon and Sly, where the ladies – white ladies – had their morning tea with scones or anchovy toast served by black waiters in immaculately-pressed white uniforms and wearing red askari hats, the type with a black tassel dangling languidly on one side.

On the outskirts of town was 'The Location', meaning the area of shanty huts to which the Africans, or 'natives' as they were then called, went home of an evening to dwell in disenfranchised penury. Few whites ever ventured to or within The Location; fewer still knew the names of the streets there; and none of the whites who I knew – and I include myself in this observation – thought it odd that this conurbation inhabited by hundreds of thousands carried such a non-descript identification. It was a hazy, dusty, smokey mass of subservience; a signal indicator of the narrow margin to which the lot of the black man was consigned in the white conscience. The Africans walked miles each way each day – to and from work; or perhaps cycled on rickety bicycles. None – or very few – owned a motor vehicle. Some rode by bus, single deck affairs that rattled their way devoid of whites.

On the other hand, the suburbs in which the whites lived were accorded names which were singularly lacking in imagination, such as 'The Suburbs' and 'Hillside' and 'North End'; though there was one concession to African heritage in naming an area 'Kumalo'. The Kumalo or Khumalo were a Zulu clan of whom Mzilikazi had been a renowned member. This particular Kumalo was a suburb inhabited in the main by relatively wealthy Jews and therefore called 'Jewmalo' by the local anti-Semites of whom the town had as fair a share as any other in the world of the redneck.

But I see that I have digressed from the urgent matter of the Watkins challenge.

I came home that afternoon, my sandwiches uneaten. On each morning that I went to school, each morning of all my school years, I was handed sandwiches neatly wrapped in butter paper; tomato sandwiches, with a pinch of salt, the envy of school boarders to whom I regularly surrendered my daily bread in exchange for a delicious meat pie from the tuck shop.

But on this day there had been no divesting of bread either to a boarder or to my stomach; my appetite had been ruined by the prospect of fisticuffs with the liver defender.

I informed my brother Henry of the prospect in store. He was then, and still is, five years older than I. He thought it amusing and didn't offer to intervene on my behalf, fully aware that David's big brother, Mine-Mervyn, was larger than Mine-Henry in the same proportion as David was to me. He suggested that I might best use the limited time available to me – both before the fight and possibly on earth – by engaging in boxing practice on my pillow. Which is what I did. I went to bed early on the pretext of a headache or stomach upset, and that night my pillow was beaten to a pulp. I had said my daily bed-time prayers in the company of my mother when, as usual, I asked the omnipotent Lord to bless my family and 'all good people', though, on this occasion, I expressly excluded the Watkins family.

Bedtime in Africa, in the days before television invaded that continent, was normally a pleasure for a nine-year-old. Evenings were spent talking with the family or listening to vinyl records or to my mother playing an old upright piano, on a panel of which was embossed in gold lettering the words 'As played by HRH Princess Ingrid of Sweden' though I wondered how the princess' piano had found its way to Bulawayo let alone to our house in Fife Street. The answer to a stern bedtime directive was to secret to bed a portable radio, place it under the covers, and there listen to 'The Day of the Triffids' or 'Journey into Space' or the broadcast of a wrestling match between Sky Hi Lee and Vic Toweel, each of whom sported cauliflower ears and a disjointed and flat nose.

This is what one did unless training for a fight of one's own scheduled for the next day. In such an event, one placed a pillow against a wall at the head of the bed, kept it aloft with one hand whilst punching it with the other, ferociously thrashing it and envisaging amidst the flying feathers the pummeled face of David Watkins, preferably with a nose as out of kilter as that of Mr Toweel.

And in the background, the mind's ear could hear, loud as the school bell, the cheers and encouragement of the class of '55, with Mrs Hayes standing in amazement as I beat to smithereens he who had once widdled on the classroom floor and who thought chopped liver was a matter of high principle.

I lay back, relishing these sweet thoughts, and thus gave way to sleep, conscious only of the thunder that rumbled in the African night.

Chapter Three

We were a family of Jews – or is it easier to say we were 'Jew*ish*'? Adding 'ish' renders it less harsh, a fact which in itself tells a tale, does it not, since 'Jew' without the 'ish' has for millennia been used as a pejorative, a fact the Jew has been consigned to suffer since whenever. Nonetheless we were very nice people really, a compliment with which the discerning non-Jew imbues the decent Jew and by decent Jew he means the Jew who is not really Jewish. Indeed, some of his best friends are Jews.

49 Fife Street wasn't in the Suburbs or in Kumalo, for our means didn't in the early years, extend to plush. It was a modest bungalow with a corrugated iron roof, situated in the town itself though on the edge of the shopping area. There was a wrought iron gate with a small hedged-in garden at the front and a verandah of highly-polished red tile flooring, bordered by a low wall with cream-coloured pillars and

French doors leading from the porch to the lounge and dining area. The front door led to a corridor with three bedrooms, a breakfast room at the far end with a bathroom off the breakfast room (strange, no?) and a kitchen. Further back still was another porch overlooking a garden which, but for a lonely banana tree, was a dust bowl which proved as fruitful an arena for child's play as my imagination conjured.

When the rain had turned the dust into mud, the mud was applied by me and my friends to the making of miniature roads, bridges, dams and streams, to be negotiated, when baked dry by the sun, by Dinky cars and farmyard toy animals that were made of lead but not, in those days, made in China. Here the neighbourhood kids would congregate to play marbles, shouting locally-coined phrases such as 'Dobs and Ningers and Take What You Get' which meant that all previous games counted for naught and the winner of the next game took everything, that is to say, everyone else's marbles. To the side of the house was a gravel driveway up and down which many a race was run on birthdays, including a chasing game called 'French and English' which had no discernible connection with either nation. The rules were simple: if a member of the English team touched the underside of an outstretched hand belonging to a member of the French team, the particular Frenchman or woman was obliged to pursue the offending Brit at high speed in an attempt to grab hold of him or her before he or she reached home base. And vice versa. If the pursuit was successful, the captured individual was at once absorbed into the other team until the depressing point at which everyone was either French or English; an unintended form of the Entente Cordiale.

In the corner of the backyard dust bowl was the chicken coop which housed the weekly Friday night chicken; not the same chicken but the one that was next in line to be souped and eaten.

At the very back of the yard were the quarters of the domestic staff though we whites called them 'Boys' Rooms', because African male adults were called 'boys' and African children 'picaneens', even to their faces whether in supposedly polite conversation or otherwise. It is an astonishing fact that the indignity visited upon a male adult when he or his colleagues were referred to as 'boy' struck so very few whites as just that – an obvious indignity. No single African to my memory ever voiced objection to his employer about the practice; I suppose it was more than his job was worth.

Here in the servants' quarters lived our excellent cook, Suze, an aged retainer of temperamental disposition, too close to whom it was never wise to venture lest the wafting beer fumes rendered one a passive alcoholic.

Suze, who sported a small white-flecked moustache, had acquired for himself a wife, Agnes, a lady of substantial proportions who propelled herself forward by alternative flicks of each sizable buttock cheek. She was our housemaid and she and Suze occupied a single bed in their quarters, an achievement which boggled even the most unimaginative of minds. They were traditionalists in their relationship, meaning that they shouted at each other from morn to night and went to the beer hall each Sunday morning in single file with the man ten yards in front to show who was boss and returned in single file in the evening with the female in front to show who was the more inebriated.

We had a gardener too, a youngish man known for his propensity to resign several times a year and to apply for leave each time his mother died. This evidenced either short recall or the fact that extended family relationships entitled one to regard all female relatives above a certain age but with a relatively close degree of consanguinity, as one's mother.

My family, in descending order of age and discipline, comprised, first, my father Ernst or – as he preferred to be called in order to place as great a distance as possible between himself and the putrid Germanic milieu from which he had escaped with my mother at the tail end of 1938 – Ernest.

Born in 1907 in the Rhine Valley, not far from Cologne, he was the youngest of six siblings and by all accounts the unruliest; an unruliness encouraged by the fact that by the age of seven, he was orphaned and spoilt rotten by his several brothers and sisters, his mother, Bertha (nee Khan), having departed this life when he was aged three and she only thirty-five and his father, Moses, dying in a bicycle mishap some five years later.

The Stock side of the family had been farmers or cattle dealers for eight generations at least. It's often assumed that Dad must have changed his surname upon arrival in Africa, perhaps to conceal his Jewish roots. But that is not so. Neither natural leanings nor history suggested to him any benefit in seeking to hide one's ethnicity. He often told me that no matter how inconvenient and disadvantageous it might seem at any point in time to acknowledge one's heritage – or, rather, this particular heritage – to hide it was a pointless and demeaning exercise, the truth and wisdom of which advice became apparent enough to me with the passage of time.

It's likely that the name, generations back, wasn't Stock. I like to believe a theory, across which I have stumbled in a text about the history of the Jews on the Rhineland, that the family was descended from a group called Sajini who fled the Spanish Inquisition to Germany and was there forced in due course, with other Jews in that cradle of civilization, to alter their names to something less Semitic. The book records the fact that in 1822 one Josef Stock settled in Lommersum and that his father was Abraham Sajini of Frimmersdorf. I say that I like to believe the theory because there is something more romantic and tanned about the Spaniard, despite his Inquisition, than ever there was about the Hun, even without his holocaust. It is in any event amusing to contemplate the fact that the Nazis latched on to Aryan qualities as the pinnacle of racial purity oblivious to the fact that the true Aryan was anything but blond and blue-eyed and was instead a swarthy Indo-Iranian.

My mother was named Gerda. Her maiden name was Daniel. Her father, Michael Daniel, born in 1882 in Drove, was a Hebrew teacher-cum-cantor, having studied at a seminary in Cologne. His was a family of ten children. He married Ida Scheyer who was from the village of Gemund and after they married, they moved to Labes in Pomerania, where my mother was born in December 1916. Edith, her sister, was born three years later. Edith was blonde and blue-eyed and was recognised as a talented pianist even at a very young age. When my mother was four, the family moved to Schlochau in West Prussia, then two years later to Pyritz and eventually back to Schlochau.

Gerda and one friend, Ruth, were the only Jewish girls in their school and when she was sixteen and Edith only thirteen or fourteen, they were forced to abandon their schooling, for the Nazis then held sway. Mom had a non-

Jewish school friend whom she could only meet in secret, and going to social events was out of the question, so she and Ruth were only able to widen their social circle by making occasional forays across the nearby Polish border.

Mom found work as an assistant to a non-Jewish dentist who was forced to discharge her, by reason of her ethnicity, after only two months. He was reluctant to do so but the law was the law and had he stood firm she would have lost her job anyway because he would have lost his.

In the country at large, shops owned by Jews were daubed and boycotted; Jews were forbidden to use trams; Jews were barred from municipal hospitals; Jews were banned from cinemas; Jews were deprived of all citizenship rights; a law was proclaimed in 1935 'for the protection of German Blood and German Honour'; Jews were taunted and beaten in the streets; rabbis were depicted sucking the blood of children (pure-bred children, that is); towns and villages were 'purged' of Jews; Jews were not permitted to be judges or civil servants or to teach or lecture; the names of Jews killed fighting for Germany in the Great War were not to appear on war memorials; Jewish children were not permitted to attend schools attended by other children; books were burned; synagogues were razed to the ground; Jews were detained in concentration camps – without trial of course; Jews were excluded from sports clubs; and even so, the Olympic Games were held in Berlin.

And all of this was well known to the world at large. The hope was expressed by the Bishop of Durham in February 1936 that the revelation of these horrors, by then well-documented and published, would 'hasten the return of sanity by making yet more vocal the protest of the civilised conscience itself'. Fat chance.

After she lost her job with the dentist, Mom kept books for a Jewish produce merchant and, whilst working for that family business, she met my father. He was on a cattle buying trip to Prussia and visited a girlfriend who, it so happened, was the daughter of Mom's employer. The girlfriend, a Fraulein Carminer, introduced Ernst Stock to Gerda Daniel and the rest is history, though one with a heavy dose, in the early years, of trauma.

At about the same time, Edith met a friend of my father, a man named Ernst Rothschild, and in January 1938, the two couples were, on consecutive days, married in ceremonies conducted by my grandfather, Michael Daniel, in Euskirchen, to which town the Daniels had had to move when Schlochau was, by decree, rendered Jew-free. 'Jew free' did not, of course, mean that the Jews were by decree accorded a modicum of freedom. It meant that the Jews had been moved out; that the place itself was free of Jews, just as one is free, after effective treatment, of a disease. This practice, too, was known to the Western world, including Mr Chamberlain who solemnly announced at one stage that Herr Hitler was a man he could do business with.

Michael had fought in the 1914-18 War. On the German side, naturally. So too had a grandson of Abraham Stock. In 1879 Abraham Stock – himself the grandson of Josef – had been awarded a local honour, translated loosely as the Chief Defender of Lommersum. Not a big deal, granted, but noteworthy. Anyway, Abraham's grandson, Alfred, fell in France in 1917 fighting for Germany's honour.

Gerda's was a disposition altogether different from that of the man with whom in January 1938 she contracted a most unlikely union. He was forceful, forthright, feisty, full of laughter though not infrequently full of rage; she was quiet, the embodiment of refinement, to whom Africa was the antithesis of European greenery and cultural excellence.

She was a beauty with jet black hair tightly held back, a small nose and an understated but immaculate sense of dress. Life for her was not all it should have been for a beautiful young woman or, for that matter, for any young woman or, come to think of it, for anyone at all, since her entire family – her father Michael, her mother Ida, her sister Edith and her niece Bela, aged three years, just three years mark you – were murdered in the camps in which the so-called Aryans advanced their notion of racial purity by shooting children and their mothers and fathers.

Dogs they left alone. Hitler liked dogs. He had a dog. He had no Jews. None he was aware of anyway. He baulked at the idea of shooting or gassing dogs. Children, yes; young children; children forcibly separated from their parents; children shot in the presence of their parents; parents in the presence of their children; children made to queue whilst they waited to be shot and saw others shot. But no dogs or puppies were shot, for there was no final solution to rid the world of dogs. Imagine the fuss that would have been caused world-wide by the shooting of dogs and puppies, six million of them, to render Europe canine-free.

I had a dog. His name was Laddie. He was a mongrel of considerable intelligence with a touch of Alsatian, though evidently not sufficient Alsatian to ensure that his ears stayed upright – hence the nickname 'Floppy' with which he was endowed by the girls of Eveline High School whom he was wont to visit each term day but, by reason of some sixth dog sense, not on weekends or holidays. Quite why Laddie loped each morning several blocks to Borrow Street to the prissiest girls' school in town, only he knew. There may have been something in the air in or about our house which by osmosis instilled in its younger male inhabitants an acute nose for the whereabouts of female gatherings, no matter how far off. Laddie was not the only one with such antennae.

My brother was (is) a dog in his own right; a lady killer to boot. He had (has) film star good looks, a fact which I found profoundly irritating. At the time of L' Affaire Watkins, Henry was fourteen or fifteen – already following in Laddie's footsteps, preening himself and disconcerted by the fact that not only had he to attend school but that the school he attended, as reluctantly as Shakespeare's snail-paced schoolboy, was an all boys' institution. Henry had (has) a sniff which to this day I cannot successfully emulate, a nonchalant sniff, also in the style of Laddie, a sniff of masculine confidence accentuated by a rehearsed droop of an eyelid. Nor could I manage my coiffure as he did with his frequent change of hair styles, and an addiction to Brylcreem and to shaving lotion at a time when he hadn't started shaving.

I had hair too (then) which I doused liberally with Pantene and shampooed so often that Dad predicted I would be bald by the time I was twelve. That didn't happen (at least not quite then), but the need to shampoo so frequently was made all the more imperative by the advent of dandruff for the eradication of which I would purloin various ointments from Mom's medicine chest, for she suffered psoriasis and was possessed, so I assumed, of every cure for afflictions of the scalp known to dermatology. Whether all the ointments were for dandruff or for wholly unrelated skin or other ailments, seemed not to matter: one of them was bound to do the trick. I rather think that in the mixture which resulted, I stumbled across a concoction which significantly increased the number of dandruff flakes that adorned my pubescent scalp and the shoulders of my school blazer. But, still, beneath the dandruff, there was a sheen to my hair which I thought becoming.

At the time dandruff entered my life, so did spots or pimples, whichever sounds less unattractive. This was an inevitable concomitant of puberty and was accompanied by parental warnings not to squeeze the offending protrusions lest my face be pockmarked for life. The remedy for that too was to be found in Mom's bathroom cupboard where I uncovered a face cream of a suitable skin-coloured hue to apply artistically to the more hideous outcrops.

Thus did vanity first encroach upon my existence and a time-consuming encroachment it proved to be. But Henry never suffered from dandruff or acne. Some magic kept him immune. I think it was his sniff.

Chapter Four

My earliest recollection is of Mr Adam's leg. It was encased in Plaster of Paris. Unsigned. I was about four. I concede at once that there are many whose earliest recollections are of greater significance than a leg in plaster but if that is how it is with me, then that is how it is. The recollection is the more remarkable because I now have no idea who Mr Adams was and he never again featured in my life.

But I remember it – the leg, I mean. If he possessed a face, I never saw it. I was too far down. We were living in a flat in Grey Street, a street parallel to Fife Street at which, you may recall, my story began and where I spent the greater part of my youth. My mind's eye retains no image of the inside of the Grey Street flat save for a large oriental rug which I used as an imaginary road complex for my Dinky cars and my toy farm animals painted with lead in the days when no-one questioned whether the lead in toys was fatal.

My cars used the roads which were formed by the borders of the carpet. The cows and sheep and the milkmaid, who carried two cans on a pole and sported one and a half arms and a blue bonnet, were corralled by the rug's central medallion pattern. This was my world: cars and cows and a milkmaid amputee and the rest was adults' legs and their shoes; often farmers' shoes – real farmers' shoes not toy ones – whose residue of cow dung and the smell thereof added to the verisimilitude of my fantasy world. How things have since changed, for now it is good form to remove one's shoes when in the house of a host, so that instead of cow dung, the air is infused with the effects of bromodosis.

And thus it was that the first words I recall uttering are, "How is your leg, Mr Adams?" Not an incisive question, I grant you, but it foretold an inquiring mind. Courteous too, not that I was interested in his leg save that, in its disadvantaged condition, it hopped all over my carpet farm and I wanted it off my land.

The flat in Grey Street wasn't my first home. I was born on 15 June 1945 in the Lady Rodwell Maternity Home which was – still is – adjoined to the Bulawayo General Hospital, a large complex of buildings in vast well-trodden gardens on the outskirts of the City, between Kumalo and Hillside.

It was there that my Uncle Alfred passed away on the same day that I was subjected to an emergency appendectomy, though I am assured that the two events were unconnected. He was the lugubrious husband of sad Selma, one of Dad's sisters and the father of my cousins Herbert and Heinz, whose singular claims to the family lexicon of strange habits will be recounted later.

The appendectomy was performed on my twelfth

birthday, a fact of which I am certain because the surgeon, Dr Baron, another stalwart of the Bulawayo Jewish community, thought it amusing to wish me happy birthday as I was succumbing to the anaesthetic on the operating table. A modern youth, less imbued than were the Rhodesian youth of the day with exemplary manners, might have responded with a signal delivered by the middle finger, but it was difficult to offer a suitable riposte, since an anaesthetic in those days was administered by means of a mask doused in ether and placed firmly over the patient's nose and mouth and I suspect that my hands were strapped to prevent ripping off the mouthpiece.

I had encountered Dr Baron previously though, as in the case of Mr Adams, I had no recollection of his face, for, in a procedure for which my consent had not been sought, Dr Baron had, in a ritual similar to that to which the biblical Abraham was subjected upon divine command, circumcised me on the eighth day after my birth and the nature of that procedure did not make for eye to eye contact, though family folklore has it that I was alert enough to aim a stream of infantile urine in his general direction.

Anyway, Uncle Alfred, a short, rotund, and quiet man barely in his sixties had a prostate problem and was undergoing surgery at the same hospital on the same day as my appendectomy but Uncle Alfred didn't wake up and I did.

The entire Stock family gathered in Bulawayo for the funeral and mourning rites: family not only from Bulawayo but from as far afield as Salisbury (as it was then called, now Harare) and Cape Town and Johannesburg.

I thought that they had come to visit me. This worried me a little since I had, until their visit, assumed that the removal of an appendix was relatively routine. Still, my brother, on instructions not to reveal to me that Uncle Alfred was no more, insisted that they had all traveled to see me; and I believed him, though I couldn't understand why so many of them were crying. I began to wonder whether it wasn't my appendix that had been removed but some vital organ.

Also in the hospital at the time was one Beverly Mathieson, a young lass who grew to be a dark haired and lithe beauty. I don't know the reason for her admission to the hospital. Whatever it was, they had had to open her up. And I still can hear her pained cries from a neighbouring ward and my mother informing me that in order to ascertain the cause of such pain, the surgeons had opened her up once again and there discovered a fly. I never thought to ask whether the fly had survived its unexpected entombment or had, whilst within Beverly's intestinal maze, suffered hypoxia and perished. Still, I'm glad to relate that Ms Mathieson, whom at that time I was determined to marry – though of this fact she was forever unaware – recovered from her unusual ordeal and now resides in a country with a smaller fly population.

In the grounds of the hospital still stands a white circular tower, open to the elements at the top. Its true function remains a mystery to me but the construction is entrenched in my memory because my parents told me that it was the repository for removed tonsils and appendixes and other surplus or diseased organs. I was minded to believe them, so whenever we drove past the hospital grounds, my eyes wandered to the tower and I imagined therein an ever-growing and fetid pile of inflamed tonsils, clipped appendixes, assorted kidney stones, a collection of prostate glands, and bundles of foreskins removed by Dr Baron, the ether dispenser and happy birthday wisher. I thought of applying to the hospital authority for the return of my one and a half tonsils which had been removed when I was aged seven and which were no doubt asphyxiating somewhere near the bottom of the tower but was dissuaded by the certain knowledge that identification – well before DNA tests were commonly available – might prove difficult. I say 'one and a half tonsils', for one of my many claims to anatomical fame is the fact that one of my tonsils grew again. I have half a tonsil on the right side of my throat, a fact I unfailingly mention each time I'm examined for quarterly pharyngitis.

Near the Bulawayo General Hospital was a medical centre known as Ingutsheni. It is now referred to as a psychiatric hospital but in the days of my youth was indelicately known as a lunatic asylum, a cruel and ignorant description by the standards of modern education and civilised understanding, but a description which nonetheless conjured in the young mind images of custodial and spartan bleakness. The name Ingutsheni was only ever whispered.

After my birth at Lady Rodwell, I was taken to spend the first year of my life on Reigate Farm, of which my father was then tenant. The owner was one William Blackie, from whom in later years Dad purchased the farm. Dad and his brother Simon had, upon first arriving in the country, farmed in Figtree, a thorny arid area about thirty miles south-west of Bulawayo. There they farmed pigs, a piece of family history which has not gone down a treat with the rabbis. The fact that the family did not eat the pigs they farmed does nothing to lower the raised eyebrows, although as far as I'm aware the biblical injunction says nothing against breeding the beasts. I do not believe that this breeding decision was born of rebellion by Dad and Simon; it must just have made good business sense at the time. Leviticus also forbids the eating of camels and rock badgers but there is no family record of camel or rock badger breeding.

The farm was called Marcedale. There, in the thorn-tree dry dust bowl of central Africa, they started their new life, on Marcedale Farm: Mom, Dad, Henry, Simon, his wife Minna and their daughter Greta. Marcedale was then owned by a Jewish family towards whom Mom and Dad held long-term bitterness for reasons which were never made clear to me, but the bitterness ran deep, eventually to be replaced by a sense of pride when, years later, Dad purchased the farm. Long after it passed from Dad's ownership, Marcedale was the subject of a land grab from white farmers in the years when Robert Mugabe's government confiscated land without compensation.

In due course, Mom and Dad moved to Reigate Farm, five miles from Bulawayo and hugged on its northern boundary by the Umgusa River, a creek more often than not bone dry. In time, the new airport – the old one was in Kumalo – was built a further seven or eight miles away from the city so that the airport road ran alongside the farm and even cut through a small section of it. On the way to the airport, take the first turning left after the Umgusa and there runs the dirt road into the farm. And close to the river, about thirty three yards from its bank, was the farm house, a rudimentary bungalow with a corrugated iron roof and a small stoep or verandah, and outside a grand tree casting its intermittent shade over a softly green lawn.

In years to come, this place was to be the heart of Dad's cattle business, to which and from which cattle were driven, to be fed and bred and sold; a dusty haven of cattle pens and cattle ramps and cattle sheds and cattle trucks and tractors and silo pits and a dairy and fields of maize and acre upon acre of bush and housing for the farm workers, a ranch where Dad might be seen wearing his off-white Stetson and sucking on a cigarette-free cigarette holder and leaning upon a shooting stick, examining his four-legged beasts sometimes close up and other times from a distance or directing operations to his long–serving staff.

And this, as I say, is where I spent the first year of my life. It was almost a very short life indeed. Family anecdote has it that when I was only a few weeks old, I was lazily and nakedly reclined in a tub of warm water on the kitchen table, there bathed by the maid, or 'nanny' as African female employees were called, I ruminating – perhaps – about the indignity visited recently upon my most private possession, she humming an African lullaby in a minor key and so engrossed in her soporific task that she failed to notice the snake which had slithered into the kitchen and which was making its way up a table leg, either to eat me or to be washed as well. As quickly as she could cry out, she took up a broom and killed the unsuspecting serpent there and then. Had we lived in China and had the Lord not forbidden us the eating of creatures that crawled on their bellies, we might have had snake soup for dinner.

The happenstance of the broom at hand should come as no surprise to those accustomed to my mother's cleaning habits. There was always a broom at hand. Quite why she ever employed domestic help, I cannot say, for she would invariably work over surfaces already cleaned and was known to test the cleanliness of other people's households by running a finger surreptitiously over the sills and mantle-pieces of the houses she visited. At this she was a master of multitasking: talking, munching a biscuit, sipping tea and softly sweeping a finger at the same time, ready to provide a report after each such visit.

Alas, it was there, on Reigate Farm, that news of a true disaster befell the family. It was there that my mother received notification from the Red Cross that her family – her parents, and her sister and her brother-in-law and their three-year-old daughter, Bela, had been murdered by the Nazis at Auschwitz.

What is one to say but to recount that stark fact? What point is there in wondering, as I do, how they met their fate? Were they dragooned into a cattle truck, these elderly innocents, these newlyweds, that child, there to pass filth-laden days in terror at the thought of what awaited them? Were they made to undress in front of goose-stepping dregs of humanity and taken to a pit and shot naked as they stood? Were they shepherded into a gas chamber? Or did they starve to death? Were they separated or did they die together? What were their last words? What were their last thoughts? And upon whom did they last set their eyes? Intensely distressing though this is, it behoves us to ask these questions and to think upon them, for they were blood and flesh and compassionate beings who had asked only to be left in peace and we disrespect them if we turn our minds away.

And the evil of holocaust denial, of the canard that it is all a fabrication to further a fraudulent Judaic design, is that it trivialises the sanctity of life itself and denigrates my mother's mother and father and sister and the child Bela and mocks the grief that their deaths and the manner of their deaths visited upon the life of my mother for every remaining day of her life.

My mother screamed and wept for weeks, until she could weep no longer. And her hair went white. And she asked, quite sensibly, so it seems to me, how there could be a God to whose glory her father had devoted his life as a teacher of religion and a composer of liturgical music. Maybe this is why she seldom went to synagogue.

I have an International Red Cross message form filled out by my mother and addressed to her father, Michael Israel Daniel. It is undated but its contents reveal that my brother had by the date of the message been born. Whether by that date my grandparents had yet been murdered, one cannot say. It is addressed to my grandfather at the village called Euskirchen in the Rhineland and the number and name of the street is 18 Adolf Hitlerstrasse.

Fancy that. Think upon it; think for one moment what went through the mind of a daughter writing a message 'not exceeding 25 words' with 'only family news allowed' to her father called Michael *Israel* at an address dedicated to Adolf Hitler. The insertion of the middle name 'Israel' was required by an Executive Order of August 1938 of Jewish men whose first names were not of Jewish origin. Women had to insert the name 'Sarah'. Just so that one wouldn't forget. Not that it was altogether easy in the circumstances to forget, even if one wished to.

The message was that November brought good health, that Henry was a little rascal and that the recipients of the message were to "Bleibt Alle gesund!", which is to say, "Keep well". Keep well indeed.

I have two more Red Cross messages, each from my

grandparents in Hitlerstrasse to my parents. The first is dated 16 December 1941, addressed to 'Mr Ernst Stock, P.O. Figtree, near Bulawayo, Southern Rhodesia, Africa'. The message reads:

'Heute wieder herzliche Grusse und Kusse Wir sind gesund Hoffentlich Ihr auch Henry ist wohl goldig. Besondere Kusse von Bela.'

It translates as: 'Today once more hearty greetings and kisses. We are well. Hopefully so are you. Henry is truly delightful. Especial kisses from Bela.'

The second is dated 22 January 1942 and says:

'Euch Lieben wieder herzliche Grusse un Kusse. Wir sind gesund. Hoffen dieses von Euch. Dicken Kuss von Bela an Henry.'

The last sentence conveys a big kiss from Bela to Henry.

Each is signed in the hand of 'Papa', 'Mutti', 'Ernst' and 'Edith' (who also signs on Bela's behalf), respectively.

It is obvious from these messages that they had received photographs of Henry who, at the end of 1941, was not far off two and that Bela, then about three, had been told of her cousin to whom she sent kisses.

The Germans murdered them all, even Bela, whose photograph, amongst a series of family photographs, I recently showed to one of my granddaughters who is aged ten. My granddaughter, a sensitive and loving girl, asked if Bela was still alive and when I said she was not, asked when and how she died. What answer, what explanation, is one to provide to a child about the wanton murder of a three-year-old? How is any innocent mind to absorb the deliberate killing of innocence itself? How, save for a lie, am I to explain why Bela never grew to enjoy childhood, never lived to marry and never lived to have children of her own? Or to see Henry to whom she had sent her kisses. Bela did not die as a result of some tragic accident or the happenstance of a disease. She died because there was a plan, sanctioned by a nation, to kill children and when they had killed this particular three-year-old child, they killed another child and another and another. They killed as many children as they could. That fact is in itself the answer to those who say that we Jews make too much of the Holocaust and that it is time we moved on.

Out of this unspeakable crime, there is a solitary consolation. It is that in the battle between the two named in the messages, Israel and Hitler, Hitler is dead and Israel lives.

Chapter Five

Until quite recently, I had lost all trace of Nehemiah Golub. I had heard that he went to America with his family, where his father became the cantor in a Brooklyn synagogue and that Nehemiah himself had become a doctor and saw combat in the Vietnam War – the American one, not the French one nor the ones with China.

Nehemiah was my best friend until we were about fourteen when, in consequence of some brouhaha over his father's employment, the Golub family left the country for the USA and that was that; for some reason, which to this day I cannot identify, we never were in touch again. I managed to track his name in due course only to discover that he had died the previous year, that he had never been a doctor but rather a lawyer and that, strangest of all, he had changed his name to Neil Corbett. What events conspired to motivate that change will, to me, remain a mystery.

We lived near one another. If one turned right out of the front gate of 49 Fife Street and walked one block along the dusty and wide frontage which ran between the garden gates and the road, past the dairy shop at the corner and to the Cecil Hotel (after you know who), there, opposite the hotel, stood Nehemiah's house, owned by the Bulawayo Jewish community. I remember the house for the utter bareness of its garden patch and for the dwelling's spartan furnishings. And here Nehemiah (Hemia for short) lived with his parents and sisters. They all had distinctly swarthy complexions; Nehemiah with tightly knit hair, his looks according to my image of Egyptians – indeed the family had lived in Cairo at one stage, which may account for that connection in my mind's eye. Even the whites of his eyes were not quite white, but showed a brownish hue; and I recall especially the stubbiness of his fingers, a physical attribute he shared with his father. Of his history I knew little, save that he was born in Potchefstroom, a predominantly Afrikaans town north-west of Johannesburg. It is the only context in which I came to know of that strange sounding dorp.

A sanitary lane separated the Golub house from the synagogue in which Cantor Golub strode his stuff, and my how he strode it! He nursed a large double chin and a high forehead atop of which, when doing his cantorial thing, he wore a black circular cantor's hat (white on high holydays) crowned with a bobble. When he sang, his voice warbled and the flap beneath his chin trembled, a sight that did much to detract the worshippers from their devotions, not that it took much to detract them. As Pavarotti employed a kerchief for his standard prop, Cantor Golub flourished a tuning fork, striking it regularly as he stood on the bimah – the celebrant's elevated platform – holding the fork to his ear and humming the note it produced to the words: "Mi Mi Mi Mi Meeee." Thus it was that the word 'Mimi' played some role in my life those days, for not only would my mother name all cats 'Mimi' but my introduction to opera was of Benjamino Gigli's rendition of 'Che Gelida Manina' from La Boheme, an aria in which Rudolfo feels the need to tell Mimi something of which she has already complained, that her tiny hand is uncomfortably cold.

Here was the centre of Jewish life in a town in the south-west of a landlocked country in the middle of Africa. It remains a source of amazement to those Jews who find themselves dispersed in the Americas and Europe or at home in Israel that there was in central Africa a thriving and observant Jewish community. What sort of crazy Jew lived in Africa? Africa was for lions and snakes and all tribes other than the Hebrew tribe; surely not a habitat for the people of the Book. So, what sort of sun-stroked Jew lived in Rhodesia? It was and remains a question prompted as much by the questioner having no clue where Rhodesia was, as by the sneaking suspicion that we deliberately chose to live in a place so distant and beridden by creepy crawlies that it was bound to be safe from the prying eyes of itinerant religious zealots.

This was not a group of whites who had left Britain as adventurers, or as economic migrants, or as Temple of Doom *meshuggeners* who desired to see the sun in the sky rather than in picture books. These were *yidden* from Russia and Lithuania and Czechoslovakia and Poland and Latvia and Germany; families torn from their roots and travelling not to the East End of London or through Staten Island to the

Statue of Liberty, but to Africa, leaving behind, more often than not, mothers and fathers and siblings whom they would, most likely, never see again; mothers and fathers and siblings who would be or had been dispossessed, then shot or gassed either by Wagner's *volk* or by those in the lands occupied by the German war machine who, with just a little push, were willing to partake, often enthusiastically, in the looting and the killing.

A hotchpotch of Jews, living in a British colony, in a town called Bulawayo, which, for them, was an unfortunate name; unfortunate for two reasons. First, it translated from Ndeble into 'Place of Slaughter' as if the Jew needed to search for such a place when every thinking *mensch* knew that, given time, slaughter would find the Jew, and, secondly, the 'w' in 'Bulawayo' posed pronunciation difficulty for the European Jew who was consigned to calling his new home 'Bulavaiyo'.

The Africans called them 'Majuta', a non-pejorative term I think, and the whites, the other whites, that is, called them whatever whites call Jews behind their backs.

To we youngsters, educated in English-speaking schools, the accents of our elders provided a source of mirth. There was Mrs Altmann whose son Alfred became engaged to an eligible lass named Phylis, an eligibility which was scarred by the fact that her newly acquired mother-in-law was in the habit of prefacing every second word with the definite article 'Ze' ('the'), so that she referred to the bride as 'Ze Phylis' thereby prompting the youth of the community to search out the newly-betrothed Alfred to congratulate him on acquiring Zephylis.

And there was Mrs Kaufman who mixed her English with her German, as did many of her contemporaries, and who was always solicitous to ascertain from a returning traveler whether he had enjoyed a good *fahrt*. And Mr Stern who would dismiss the complaints of the frequently disgruntled customers of his bicycle shop – a shop from which he also, incongruously I thought, supplied the youth with condoms – with a resonant cry: "Ven err not like it, kan err lump it."

The synagogue stood at the corner of 3rd Avenue and Abercorn Street, a large white building with cream pillars to the front facade and a Star of David adorning a stained glass panel under the eaves. Here we congregated each Friday evening and Saturday morning, week after youthful week, amidst dark wood-panelled seats with seat lids under which one placed prayer books and prayer shawls. Here was demonstrated the huge advantage conferred by the orthodox requirement that men be separated from women. The assumption behind this separation is that men might be distracted from their multi-purpose prayers – prayers for peace, for rain, for a long life, prayers of awe and prayers of penitence – by the sight of a skirt or thoughts of the cleavage that palpitated beneath a blouse. But to youthful supposed worshippers, with imaginations dominated by the exigencies of puberty and its afterglow, the gathering of all the females in one area inevitably dictated an effect which was the converse of that intended by the rabbis. The women were consigned to the gallery upstairs, looking down upon the men wrapped in their prayer shawls and, ostensibly, in spirituality.

The men – the family men, or most of them – were indeed engaged from time to time in prayer. But each male youth had his gaze fixed other than in his prayer book. His gaze was fixed aloft, scanning the local talent and whispering his analysis either to himself or to his compadres, perhaps to be snapped out of his trance by an irate father asking whether he thought that he had come to synagogue solely to look at girls. To which there was but one honest answer. The story went round – probably apocryphal – that one quick-witted youth with a death wish, clipped on the ear by his father for sacrilegious inattentiveness on the Day of Atonement and directed to have atonement in his heart, muttered *sotto voce* to his buddy: "I have atonement in my heart, I really do; but in my pants it is *simchas torah*"(a festival of rejoicing).

On Saturday mornings, and before Nehemiah and his family left the country, I would sit, not with Dad and Henry but next to Nehemiah who had requisitioned a seat immediately below the bimah where his father stood conducting the service. I suspect that Nehemiah chose that seat because its position was out of his father's line of sight. This had two advantages: the first, that we could whisper to each other without his father knowing; the second, that Nehemiah, a most conscientious student, could study for his exams whilst pretending to pray.

I did not always sit downstairs with the men. There was a choir loft above the *aron hakodesh*, the ark where the Torah scrolls were kept, and I was for some years a member of the choir. The loft was out of sight of the congregation, the choristers shielded from view by a curtain which we might occasionally move and inch or two to peek at the congregants below. There a group of men and boys gathered most Friday nights, to welcome the sabbath tunefully, under the baton of Mr Levin, an elderly narrow-faced gentleman who had some difficulty maintaining discipline.

I had, in those days, if I say so myself, a rather fine voice for which reason I was regularly assigned to sing solos, as had Henry in earlier days. Many of the compositions were by the German composer Lewandowski with whose liturgical music my parents were familiar, so their pleasure in hearing their sons sing in synagogue was enhanced by the warm memories, though tinged with sadness, which that familiarity aroused.

On high holydays, such as the Day of Atonement, the ranks of the choir were augmented by the addition of some female singers, including a Mrs Middledorf, a formidable lady with a powerful soprano trill, whom we tried to mimic when she wasn't present, thereby driving Mr Levin close to breakdown. My vocal contributions were lent extra kudos by the duets I performed with Cantor Golub, I in my lofty perch, he on the bimah with his tuning fork.

One member of the choir was Dr Kibel, who was possessed of a bass voice which was almost as resonant as that of Paul Robeson. Dr Kibel was a pediatrician, perhaps the only one in Bulawayo and to whom I was once hauled to see whether he might cure me of what was then referred to as a nervous stomach. It was a memorable visit, quite unlike any I have ever experienced, for he tried to hypnotise me. He must have been on some hypnotherapy course for pediatricians and thought that my ailments would be susceptible to cure by this method. It didn't work, mainly because I convulsed with laughter at the first attempt, a habit I was to repeat throughout my childhood and into adulthood when placed in a situation which required solemnity. The episode didn't adversely affect our choral cooperation, though I was always on the lookout for any hint of hypnotic vibrations in the choir loft.

Few of the young of our community were renowned for their sporting prowess and none for technical skills, though there was one Jewish electrician and one Jewish plumber, each of whom was kept busy enough attending to the short circuits and leaking pipes which most of the congregants couldn't recognise or diagnose let alone repair. What really mattered was academic achievement, as it had through the ages, for therein lay the passport to security and relative independence from the vagaries of gentile largesse. Which is not to say that there were no sportsmen amongst us. Young Margolis played rugby for the school. So did Rufus Gruber. And the very tall and thin Basil Katz played tennis for the country, no less. We looked upon Basil as an oddity: what sort of *mensch* took pleasure in hitting a ball back and forth across a net?

In two rare specimens, however, there resided the combination of athleticism and academic success: Freddie Goldstein, who was an ace cricketer as well as a genius, and Jock Orkin, who was a weightlifter, built like a rock and of academic excellence too. How could this be? What freak of ethnic concatenation conspired to produce a scholar who could also hit a cricket ball or lift a heavy weight?

Which brings me back to the pending fight with Watkins about which the reader has anxiously been scouring these pages for a denouement.

The denouement lies in the community mindset of which I now speak. Jewish boys simply did not don boxing gloves. We did not drink beer. We did not go partying on Friday nights, for the sabbath eve was for candle lighting, matzo balls and chicken soup. We did not start meals without breaking bread. We did not rise from the table until after a fulsome grace even though it seemed to go on endlessly. And we did not fight each other in the school hall.

At any rate, that is what Myra Watkins decided when she discovered that Mine David was going to make mincemeat instead of chopped liver and that I was to be the meat. She knew me only as 'Shtok' and was given to addressing me in benign shrieks, most often when she saw me at bar mitzvah or wedding receptions for which she catered and concluded that I was not eating enough. "Shtok!" she would bellow. "Eat! Eat!"

Anyway, it turned out that she instructed Mine David that on no account was he to go through with the slaughter. I was thinner, she most accurately remarked, than any chicken she had cooked and she had cooked many chickens. I would probably be killed. Now that I think of it, she probably issued her prohibition less to protect me than to ensure that Mine David wouldn't be charged with manslaughter.

So David reported to me, rather sheepishly it seemed to me, that his mother had forbidden the fight. I thought, momentarily, of suggesting to him that this was an excuse on his part but, in the event, and without too much dithering, I resiled from offering this chutzpah-laden suggestion, lest David change his mind. I accepted the decision with appropriate feigned grace and went to the toilet nearest class 3A where, in relief, both in mind and in technicolour, I threw up.

Chapter Six

In due course, circumstances dictated a move from the farm to the apartment in Grey Street, the place where Mr Adams was to show off his plastered leg. Quite what motivated the move no-one told me: I wasn't consulted. Perhaps it was feared that the distraught mate of the snake which had wanted to eat me might inveigle its way into the farm house to exact its revenge; or perhaps it was the fact that Henry was required to commence his schooling. Years later, Henry starred as the headmaster in a school production of 'The Happiest Days of Your Life' which demanded considerable thespian skills on his part since school was never on his list of a thousand things he wanted to do before he died.

Henry went to Baines Junior school, in the suburb named North End because it was at the north end of town. It was a mixed school, not as to race of course, but as to gender which goes a long way to explain the references in Henry's school reports to his failure to concentrate. Sending Henry, even at a young age, to a mixed school was akin to sending a healthy growing dog to a kennel where the main fare was T-bone steak. His concentration on work was in inverse proportion to his concentration on girls. Since my parents thought that academic effort was more important than preparing for relationships in later life, the availability of an all male secondary school, when he reached the appropriate age, was a godsend.

It was a hallmark of the reports from Baines School that each was entitled a 'Terminal Report'. Henry treated them as such, namely with the foreboding that accompanies incurable illnesses. Envelopes must in those days – in that neck of the colonial woods, at any rate – have been scarce, for reports were folded with the address written on the back of the report under 'O.H.M.S' – On His Majesty's Service – though His Majesty, then King George VI, did not himself post the letters.

Henry also attended the Louis Landau Hebrew School. Who Louis Landau was no one thought to inquire. But the Hebrew School evidenced an afternoon commitment for all children of the community two or three days a week. Secular school commenced early, finished at about lunch time, leaving afternoons for sport. Or for Hebrew School, housed in a building across the road from the synagogue.

At Hebrew School, one was taught, well, Hebrew, although it tended to be biblical Hebrew rather than the modern language, and one was also taught to write Hebrew characters; read and written from right to left, with characters having no semblance to Latin script. The courses equipped one to read, though not understand, prayers and little else.

Henry did well at Hebrew School. Dated 9 December 1948, the third term of that year, when Henry was aged eight years, his Hebrew School report remarked, surprisingly, that his conduct was good, that his dress was very good – as if that mattered – and that he was keenly interested.

So what the hell had happened to the lack of concentration which was his predominant claim to notoriety at Baines School? This puzzles me. Either the maker of the report confused Henry for someone else or there were no blonde girls in the Hebrew class, which is much more likely. No blondes, no distraction.

I started school at Coghlan Kindergarten. It was a girl's primary school situated in Borrow Street, a block away from Milton Junior School. Although the primary school was for girls, the kindergarten was for little boys as well.

School did not then seem to me to be a sound proposition and I protested with all the tears I could muster. I was awash with tears. I preferred the company of my lead cows on my carpet farm or the pick-up sticks and tiddlywinks I played there. So, with all the ploys I could conjure, I sought to engineer an outcome which would preserve this self-absorbed life of mine; yet to no avail. I can recollect none of my Coghlan School teachers which is no surprise since I only ever saw them through the mist of tears, like driving through an English day's rain with the windscreen wipers swishing aside one stream of miserable water only to be deluged at once with another. But crying didn't achieve the objective.

So I tried shamming. In later school years, I became quite adept at shamming. It occasionally worked. Headaches, migraines, vomit caused by drinking salt water, and faking yellow fever after learning that there was such a disease and that its incidence of fatality was high. So too, I managed not only the symptoms but the actuality of dysentery by raiding the pantry for copious quantities of prune juice. When that ruse was discovered, I contrived constipation by taking no fluids at all and even rejected my favourite liquid of all, which was chicken soup, the cure-all in any Jewish home for any illness. When the constipation was confirmed by considered and worried parental examination of my stool in a potty, I was taken to Dr David, who had rumbled me ages ago and recommended an enema, not of chicken soup but of hot water, which was not quite the same at all. The threat itself cured the constipation. I surrendered and went to school.

There, I suddenly took on a gregarious mien, which I have ever since retained. I chatted away. I did whatever they asked. The school report which was issued next after my return from constipation-induced absence suggested that although I was doing well and was a splendid conductor of the percussion band, I was apt to 'waste time chattering'. 'Yet, even so,' remarked Miss Gibb, 'there has been a most gratifying change in Frankie. He is far more confident and will tackle things without being upset.' Well, dear Miss Gibb, had they looked into your potty and threatened to flush warm water up your backside to evacuate all the hard poops, there would have been a gratifying change in you too.

Thus cleansed of fear and of supposed ailments, I took avidly to reading books such as 'Watch the Pony Grow!' about a pony who, so it seemed to me from the illustrations, remained a pony even when he was an adult, and 'The Adventures of Nicholas Thomas on Timothy's Farm' about such animals as Peter Piper Piggy-Wig whose mother, Mrs Piggy-Wig, was an unusual pig since she always had a headache, which no doubt accounted for the fact that Peter Piper Piggy-Wig had no piglet siblings. It also contained a politically suspect account of Timothy Twopence who was given to pulling the hair of a girl called Penelope at which she protested so they agreed to play catch instead. A less well-leafed volume was a book of pastimes such as bird watching, collecting moths and butterflies, collecting wild flowers, visiting birds' nests, and 'how to recognise trees' which made me wonder what sort of sheltered person couldn't recognise a tree when he saw one. I still have the book. I have never read it.

These were times well before television intruded upon the lives of Rhodesians, so there was time to do what children are supposed to do, which is to play games and read and enjoy the outdoors, the last of which was the natural consequence of living in a country blessed with an amplitude of space and extraordinarily fine weather.

Christmas wasn't celebrated in our household, not surprisingly since it was seen as a religious festival the preserve of another faith. In that non-observance, we were not, amongst the Jewish community, unique. Christmas wasn't marked and Easter not observed although the latter seemed to coincide with the Passover with remarkable frequency, well before it came home to me that the coincidence of the Last Supper and Passover was not a coincidence at all.

But there was, in our family, a solitary concession to Christmas which I still recall. Mom felt guilty one year that all my non-Jewish friends were excited at the prospect of their Christmas stockings and she came to the conclusion that no harm would be done if I too hung out a stocking to be filled whilst I slept through the night of 24th December. And it was done and I was much thrilled by the anticipation and the result. Whether Father Christmas indeed visited me in central Africa that hot summer's night is open to conjecture, but I thought he did and no one in the community was ever the wiser. What's more, no lightning struck our house that month or in the months which followed.

Chapter Seven

To the Louis Landau Hebrew School – the one which deemed Henry to be well-dressed – we were expected to repair several afternoons a week. I say 'expected' because attendance was honoured more in the breach than in the observance. Some attended outside the building whilst the lessons progressed inside but whether inside or outside, even the most angelic and studious boys and girls, with the exception of the Golub and Yesorsky children, underwent an instantaneous metamorphosis on arrival for, in general, they ran riot. The Golub father was the cantor and the Yesorsky father was the rabbi so their children were forgiven for not misbehaving.

The Hebrew teacher was named Mr Nenklebaum. I doubt whether he had a first name; if so, it certainly wasn't a Christian name. 'Nenklebaum' was a mouthful so we called him 'Ninkybum', though not, I am relatively sure, to his face.

He lodges still in my memory. He had a Neanderthal bearing. His deeply furrowed forehead protruded like that of a Neanderthal and his arms swung as low as that of a Neanderthal and the other facet of his anatomy which significantly protruded was his fulsome upper lip which enwrapped itself over his bottom lip as if glued there slowly to be unglued when it was his turn to shout. I never discerned his nationality but he was foreign for sure and spoke with a strong accent which originated, I imagine, from some nondescript village in Eastern Europe. How this poor man came to find himself in central Africa remained a mystery about which none of us bothered to inquire.

Life for Ninkybum was hell. He had the thankless task of attempting to teach and maintain discipline over youngsters who had no interest in what he was teaching and who found his attempts at injecting order and civility an irresistible challenge to be as unruly as was possible. Silence never reigned in his classroom; the only thing that rained were paper aeroplanes. The litany of excuses for not completing homework assignments would have made Baron Munchausen proud. His rages were frequent and colourful; colourful in the sense of the many vibrant shades of purple which his contorted face managed to exude.

He wore a small yarmulke on his troubled head, insufficiently fastened to his few head hairs, and the challenge to dislodge this head covering reached its apotheosis when one of our number so positioned Ninkybum's desk, which stood on a raised platform, that when he leaned on his desk to make a biblical point, the desk fell and he with it and the yarmulke at almost the same time. This was not funny, of course, and someone got into trouble for it but there was a limit to the effective punishment available, for expulsion was a threat that carried few terrors.

He occasionally threatened hell, fire and damnation, even though heaven and hell did not occupy much of a place in our religious teachings. But there were defences against his threats. One of the most extraordinary was flourished by a lad – still alive to my knowledge and living a respectable life in London – in the form of his, the pupil's, dog. The lad, of bold disposition, brought his dog to Ninkybum's class, not so that the hound could be tutored in the finer points of the Kabbalah, but to guard him against the certainty of a punishment which in those days included the chance of a cane or ruler across the palm or even the backside. The dog sat itself obediently next to the pupil but failed miserably to fulfil its deterrent role, for the sight of Mr N's enraged face, with its curled lip, its purple hue and bulging front cranial subcutaneous veins so frightened the poor animal that it whimpered once and left the room, swiftly and shamefully conceding defeat.

For these many trespasses, it was fruitless to seek Mr Nenklebaum's forgiveness; fruitless because Christian forgiveness was, by definition, not on our menu and it would be fruitless now belatedly to seek his forgiveness not only because he is no longer likely to be alive but also because our treatment of him was, to tell the truth, the whole truth and nothing but the truth, unforgivable.

The milestone to which every young *kaka* looked forward was his bar mitzvah – 'kaka' being the anally dismissive term by which we were called by our older brothers and our fathers when they wanted to convey their opinion that we were little shits of no significance. When I say 'looked forward', it is not to be assumed that the bar mitzvah was anticipated with unqualified eagerness. But, all in all, it was a big deal.

On the plus side, it was the occasion upon which each member of the family and almost each member of the sizable community felt obliged to display a degree of largesse in gifts to mark the occasion.

Almost every gift was accompanied by a card which unimaginatively said: 'To Frankie, On the Occasion of His Bar Mitzvah'. Sometimes telegrams were sent: 'Mazeltov on the occasion of your bar mitzvah.' Or telegrams to the parents: 'Mazeltov and may you have many years of *naches*' – by which was meant, not many years of Mexican tortilla chips, but, as the Yiddish word *naches* portends, many years of pleasure from your son. In this context 'many years of pleasure' in turn meant many years of the sort of behaviour which every decent Jewish parent is entitled to expect from a decent Jewish boy and, if further and better particulars of decent behaviour were needed, it comprised being studious, becoming a doctor or, if averse to blood, a lawyer and, above all, marrying within the faith.

So much for the good wishes.

As for the gifts themselves, these too were by and large of the predictable variety: a Parker '51 fountain pen perhaps or a tie pin or, from those who did not want to go shopping, a cheque. And from the local hypochondriac, one might count on a copy of Collins' 'Home Doctor' and since the congregation possessed more hypochondriacs than any other sect in the country, the chance of receiving several copies was high, though I should not mock hypochondria for in that realm my family members were the undisputed exemplars – if Her Majesty the Queen were given to according honours for services to hypochondria, all the Stocks would be Knights of the Garter.

From the non-Jews came less predictable gifts: Churchill's 'History of the English Speaking Peoples' first published in 1956, which was a godsend to those whose bar mitzvahs fell in the few years thereafter; Van Loon's 'History of Mankind'; H G Wells' 'History of the World'; a wrist watch, perhaps; or, my favourite, a catapult.

And, inevitably, a signet ring from my Aunt Selma whose imagination never stretched beyond signet rings for all her nephews on landmark occasions. I lost mine a year or two later on a beach in Cape Town when I was much taken by the idea of throwing it over a shoulder – mine – to see where it landed. Predictably, it landed in the fine white beach sand. Deep down, I think, for though I conducted a methodical search reminiscent of a grid search for a missing person thought to be dead in a large field, the ring remains missing. I imagine it to have been swept back into the Indian Ocean, carried along the West Wind Drift past Western Australia and up the Augulhas Current to the coast of Sri Lanka, there discovered on the beach at Gall by a distracted fisherman picking his nose who sold it to a Tamil rebel who may be reading this now, in which case, I would be grateful for its return.

On the negative side, the less attractive aspect of bar mitzvahs were the preparatory lessons which spread themselves over a year. They were divided into two parts: the learning of the portion of the Law and of a portion of the Prophets which were to be performed in a hopefully tuneful display in the synagogue in full view of family and other congregants and, the second, learning about the tenets of the religion itself – the significance of the high holy days, the detail of ritual observances, reading Hebrew and so on, all of which culminated, shortly before performance day, with the bar mitzvah examination.

The theory was that passing the examination, an oral trial by ordeal, was a condition precedent to the staging of the bar mitzvah ceremony – the performance in the synagogue – itself. Such was the theory, that if one failed the examination, one said bye-bye to the ceremony. But few candidates feared that possibility and that was because no one ever failed. It didn't happen and what is more, it couldn't happen. No matter how feeble the exam performance, failing the candidate was unthinkable, for cancelling the ceremony meant no celebration and no celebration meant sending all the relatives back to their homes, far flung homes in many instances, cancelling the post-service reception at the Guild Hall across the road from the synagogue, throwing away the chopped liver exquisitely prepared by Myra Watkins, cancelling the expensive dinner dance at the Victoria Hotel, returning all the bar mitzvah presents, and then re-booking it all for one year hence in the hope that the failed candidate would apply himself sufficiently to pass next year. So you get the point – it could not happen. And since it could not happen, no one bothered studying for it.

My examination was conducted before a three man panel: Rabbi Yesorsky, Mr Kaplan and a third whose identity I forget. Mr Kaplan was married to Mrs Kaplan. Mrs Kaplan, first name Sadie, was a mauve lady. In my mind's eye I see her as entirely mauve for she wore mauve hats, mauve shoes, mauve dresses and, for all I know, mauve undergarments. In addition to this claim to the idiosyncratic, she persistently smiled, even when imparting tragic news. She couldn't help it, I suppose: maybe the glare cast by the reflection of her mauveness off sunlit pavements was such as to cause a painful grimace that resembled a smile. And she talked incessantly, the relevance of which is that Mr Kaplan, one of the examiners, was a quiet man; not surprising really, what with Sadie's mauve soliloquies. Mr Kaplan asked no questions. The rabbi did.

Mom decided that she wished to be present at the oral examination for, after all, it wasn't often that the daughter of a Hebrew teacher was given the opportunity to witness her son's examined display of religious knowledge. My objections were assumed to be a mere display of modesty which only served to make her more determined to be there. It was not a good idea. My performance was sufficiently abysmal that my own mother was consigned, not so surreptitiously, to hold aloft ten fingers when I did not know what event was commemorated by the festival of Pentecost. The examiners pretended not to see this breach of the rules though, in hereby confessing it, I am at risk of being stripped of my bar mitzvah credentials and, therefore, of reverting to boyhood, for according to Jewish tradition, the bar mitzvah signals, at the age of thirteen, the passage to manhood, which may have been true enough in biblical times when life spans were short but which is by modern standards an obvious nonsense. Each bar mitzvah 'boy' was regularly assured that the ritual signified the assumption by him of all the responsibilities of manhood, of fully fledged members of the community. That we were not nearly of marriageable age, indeed barely into puberty, that we had most of our formal education ahead of us, that none of us had training in the ways of the world, that spots had not yet appeared on our faces, was all not to the point it seems: we were, overnight, supposedly turned from saplings into adults and having thus been transformed, we went home to our mothers and fathers and our games of marbles, unencumbered by mortgages, wives, children of our own, bank accounts, jobs, or the vote.

The lessons for my bar mitzvah, whereby I was trained to sing a lengthy portion of the prophets (in Hebrew), took an unusual turn. They became part of a power struggle between cantor and rabbi. Officially it was the rabbi – or rabbit, as my Chinese secretary of later years would call the holder of that office – who taught bar mitzvah boys their prescribed portions. But the cantor's son was my best friend and the cantor decided that the melody taught me by the rabbi was not a sufficient vehicle for my fine voice; so I had lessons from the rabbi at his house in the presence of the rabbi's wife, a kindly lady of buxom proportions, and I had lessons for the same portion but with a different melody from Cantor Golub, in the presence of his equally buxom wife, each tutor vying for the acclaim that would vicariously come his way.

This made for a problem. I could not at one and the same ceremony simultaneously perform both melodies and one of these two stalwarts of religion was going to be severely perplexed on the big day when hearing me sing a different tune to the one which he had taught me for months. The question was whose to choose and how to explain to the other what had transpired and why.

A week or so after the bar mitzvah examination and a few days before the ceremony, my family gathered from different parts of South Africa and Rhodesia. It was June 1958. I proudly sported a watch given to me by a farmer friend of my father, Major Errington. The watch was engraved on the back panel with my name and the incorrect date of my bar mitzvah.

The most vocal of the family visitors was Aunt Emmy whose home was in Cape Town. She was the matriarch of the family, the eldest of the line of siblings of which Dad was the youngest; the matriarch because their parents had passed away by the time Dad was seven and she had assumed the role of his mother. She was short and round, harboured a mischievous twinkle in her eyes and spoke in a high pitch with broken English. Who could blame her for looking up the German word 'mandeln' when researching the English for 'almonds' and, alighting on the second meaning of the self-same word in German, asking a confused sweetshop assistant for a packet of tonsils.

She had the notion, which she expressed with shrieks of delight, that I had my eye on her granddaughter Maureen, then aged about twelve, a notion well founded though it was not my first crush. The first was when I was eight, another cousin though more distantly removed, next to whom I sat at a concert so that the pink fluff from her jumper stuck to my shirt: she was killed years later by the stray bullet of a gangster in Johannesburg. From Maureen I stole a kiss – a peck, I suppose; her husband (a later acquisition of course) has recently had a heart attack in Florida – I hope that this revelation, should he read it, will not strain another valve.

The great day arrived. I wore a suit. I sported a white yarmulke and a new prayer shawl. I sat with Dad and Henry and other male members of the family in one of the front rows of the men's downstairs section, for this was the bar mitzvah tradition. My mother and the rest of the female contingent were upstairs, opposite, and we spent much of the morning smiling at and mouthing messages to them.

I was duly summoned to the bimah, there to join Cantor Golub on one side of me, and the Reverend Yesorsky on the other, and to sing my portion of the Law and from the Prophets. There was a platform for me so that I might be seen above the height of the reading desk and so that I might see what I was supposed to be reading. Not that that was necessary for I had by then rehearsed the portions so frequently that I knew them by rote.

I was in fine form yet I recall my brother gesticulating from below that I should look at the torah from which I was meant to read, rather than search the faces of my family and friends for wonderment and approval. Henry had decided, a week or two before the bar mitzvah, to submit himself to a crew cut in consequence of which defiant act, just when the eyes of the world would be on our family, he was in Coventry.

The conflict between the melody taught to me by the rabbi and that by the cantor was resolved by a momentary inspirational spark, a solution which only came to me, as if divinely ordained, as I reached the crucial passage where the rabbi's tune required a soft and low note and the cantor's a strong, voluble and prolonged trill : I simply sang flat, to the puzzlement of both. Thus was honour saved.

Stage two of the ceremony entailed standing in front of the holy ark above which hangs an encased eternal flame or, rather, a lamp which gives the appearance of a flame, and reciting the bar mitzvah prayer which begins with the undertaking that 'on this solemn and sacred day which marks my passage from boyhood to manhood, I humbly raise my eyes unto thee, and declare, with sincerity and truth, that henceforth I will keep thy commandments'.

I am not sure that at the point of intoning that promise I was aware that there were so many commandments to keep; 613 of them by all accounts and some of them easier than others to observe.

To be fruitful and multiply lends itself to achievement, all being well, as do the injunctions not to eat the worm in a fruit and not to castrate a man or a beast or a fowl. It is, however, permissible, albeit within certain strict bounds, to slaughter beasts and fowl – being careful in the process to leave the genitals alone. The notion that one is duty bound to love the stranger is right there amongst the 613, well before the time of Jesus, but this duty to love all and sundry is not to be taken as going so far as marrying a gentile. One commandment of particular note is the prohibition against borrowing on interest since to do so makes the lender in breach of the covenant not to lend at interest. This is a commandment which has not met with general approbation or observance and citing it to my bank manager has invariably proved futile.

Then followed the sermon by the rabbi, directed by him from his pulpit at the newly admitted bar mitzvah 'boy' who is required by tradition to stand before him in splendid isolation and who listens to not a word of the priest's exhortations or to his pronouncement that here at last is a young man who will be a blessing to his proud parents and a future pillar of the Bulawayo Hebrew Community.

Lastly comes the presentation of the prayer book, donated by the Louis Landau Hebrew School, the prayer book of the United Hebrew Congregation of the British Empire. I still have it.

I also still have the typed speech I wrote and delivered at the reception that evening at the Victoria Hotel. It is typed on my Dad's letter head of the time: 'E. Stock. Friesland and Ranching Cattle Riding Horses and Mules'.

The speech is a *locus classicus* of its kind, as full of standard platitudes as might be imagined. 'For years,' it began, 'I have been looking forward to this great day.' What on earth could any thinking audience make of that, save that it was a gross exaggeration? And then, words of thanks to my parents 'for everything you have done for me up to now,' with the implication that merely because they had done everything for me *up to now*, that did not guarantee that they would do everything for me thereafter. Then this: 'Reverend Yesorsky, I thank you for the inspiring words addressed to me in the synagogue. They have made a big impression upon my mind and I shall do my very best to remember them.'

Those two sentences embraced three stark untruths: first, I had heard the same words addressed to all previous celebrants and so they did not inspire; secondly, because I was not listening, they had made no impression upon me; and thirdly, as for remembering them, by the time of the speech's delivery I had forgotten every word.

Chapter Eight

That every family is unique is self-evident, but not every family is bizarre, still less is every member idiosyncratic. My family qualified on each of those grounds.

Dad was obsessively superstitious and the family as a whole was burdened with every ailment known to the medical profession: angina pectoris, angst-induced spastic colons, wheezy asthma, air induced hay-fever, amoebic dysentery, yellow fever, highly dangerous influenza, orchestral flatulence, post-tonsillectomy tonsillitis, water-borne bilharzia, leaking heart valves (all of them), not-so-transient transient ischemia, non-specific global amnesia of the specific variety, pre-traumatic stress disorder, post-appendectomy appendicitis and universal functional overlay – the last of which is psychiatric talk for a fertile imagination.

And manners. Manners were strongly stressed. Good manners that is. Not a bad thing, you might well say and indeed it stood us in fine stead as time went by. But some rules went too far. So, for example, it was bad form not to look people in the eye, even when one was not engaged in conversation and which in any event when one was aged, say, five, was difficult when the eye belonged to a six-footer. "Look Mr Hochstetter in the eye!" my father would insist, which, in the case of Mr Hochstetter was painfully counterproductive for Mr Hochstetter was a copious smoker of fat cigars, so that looking him in the eye would have challenged the most resolute of chimney sweeps. I only ever saw him behind billows of smoke and to this day I am not sure how many eyes he possessed.

And haircuts had to be short. Anything else was a sign of dissolution, degeneration and homosexuality, the last of which in that age was regarded with less enlightenment and more cruel prejudice than in present times. The irony is that I then had much hair and was made to have less, whereas now I have less but cannot have more. Shit happens.

Why they called me Frank when my father was called Ernest, only they knew; no doubt the juxtaposition of the names was lost on them given that their native tongue was German, though they tried as best they could to divest themselves of any fact that reminded them of that background. Home cooking possessed much that was, in truth, German. Strudel. Apple sauce with everything. Senf (mustard) sauce. Boiled brisket. Red cabbage. Sour cabbage. Sweetbreads, which my friends believed to be bull's testicles and of which, accordingly, they refused to partake. The paternal insistence, however, was that all this was Jewish cuisine. German, never.

Mom had greater success than did my father in shedding outward manifestations of foreignness for she was scholastically inclined, widely read, and prided herself in grammatical exactitude. Unpopular though it was for her to say so at home, she occasionally and in wistful moments revealed a recollection of the poetry of Schiller and Goethe. During all her years in Africa, she yearned for the culture and the scenery of Europe.

Ernest came to the country in January 1939. He had traveled with a brother, Simon and with Simon's wife, Minna and their daughter, Greta and with my mother too. They came by sea. The plan had been to join an advance party established by Emmy and her husband Otto and another brother Siegfried, a man of immaculate dress taste, all of whom had put down roots in Cape Town, but by 1939 South Africa had closed its doors to refugees.

Dad was born in a small rural village near Cologne. His parents were cousins of one degree or another, over which fact the family tends to gloss for fear that by mentioning it we might the more readily be recognised for the lunatics we are. By all accounts, Dad as a child was a handful of mighty proportions. So determined was he from an early age to skip school in order to be in the preferred company of horses and cows and the smell of their manure and so unruly was he to achieve that purpose, that he was in due course sent away to school. He thereupon and with malice aforethought smeared his school referral report with butter conscientiously scraped from the sandwiches given him by his sister Emmy for the journey, wherefor he was expelled from the school of his destination as soon as he arrived. In the Deutschland of the second decade of the twentieth century, there was no such thing as a quiet word on parents' evening.

The Stock siblings were strong characters, each with

expressive eyes, heavy bushy eyebrows, muscular jaws, and hyper-active minds. They were mischievous, hot tempered, obsessive worriers, had keen business acumen (a quality I have not inherited), fertile imaginations (I have), fervent ambition, quiet pride in their achievements, a preference for practical over academic experience, smart dress codes and hypochondria.

Whether I too am a hypochondriac I leave to my detractors to say. At the date of writing – for the thing is a moveable feast and tomorrow may bring new problems – I have a scratch on my left eye caused when playing with my shih-tzu dog, Brian; a hairline fracture of an ankle bone occasioned by a trip in a ditch at my elder son's wedding, an excusable mishap were it not for the fact that at the time I was cold sober; renal impairment caused by over-consumption of anti-inflammatory tablets for migraines; a stent somewhere in my heart; internal scratches occasioned by the second of my four colonoscopies; something called a Schatzki's ring which prevents food from going down as smoothly as it should; a pituitary adenoma, which sounds suitably serious; and haemorrhoids. In the twelve months preceding the writing of this chapter, I have had three MRIs, an endoscopy, a panendoscopy and a bone marrow extraction, all performed under anaesthetic because in the case of the MRIs, I am claustrophobic and, unless knocked out by the soporific drug which killed Michael Jackson, I will press the emergency button within three seconds of entering the tube wearing the type of mask designed for the psychopath in 'Silence of the Lambs'.

I confess to haemorrhoids, not to inject lavatorial unpleasantness into this account, but because a wag of a South

African doctor, a friend of my brother, thought it amusing to scare me a little by saying, as I was curled in the foetal position to facilitate an examination by him of my haemorrhoids, that the delay in commencing the examination was because he could not get the zip of his trousers undone.

I visit my general practitioner once every two months or so. I say 'my' practitioner advisedly for, given the frequency of my consultations with him, he has no financial need of other patients. I see him for anticipated influenza, for outbreaks of sweating occasioned by the fear rather than the reality of malaria, and for him to examine whatever new spot appears on my body in order, at my insistence, to remove the cancerous blemish before it has even considered becoming cancerous. He removes one wart per visit, submits it for biopsy, stitches the wound and then sees me again for my imagined resulting infection.

Dad lived until he was eighty-seven. This was well beyond anything one might have expected given the history of his medical battles. He suffered two prime ailments. First, angina pectoris, of which he convinced himself whenever we went on holiday and second, the spastic colon to both of which I have already referred. Every male member of the family was/is possessed of a spastic colon, which is to say, a colon which goes into spasm at the most inconvenient of times and places and for no apparent reason, although I think it has to do with tension, tension-induced shouting, and panic. How the condition manifested itself is unnecessary for me to relate in any refined company, save to recall a disastrous boat trip on a river in Mozambique when the tour guide's running commentary was drowned out by Dad's insistence that the excursion be cut short to allow for running of a different kind.

If none of this is odd, my father's superstitions were. They were odd and numerous and their rigorous observance by the entire household was insisted upon.

No music was allowed before noon. No radio, no humming, no whistling. Anything resembling music before noon foretold – nay, guaranteed – ill luck. I was familiar with many superstitions: do not walk under ladders; the number thirteen was unlucky; the name of the Scottish play was never to be articulated. But no music before noon? I have to this day no idea of the origin of this lunacy but it was an injunction we all obeyed whilst in his company. We were bemused by it but the prohibition was religiously observed. Even Isaac, the man who drove my father's car, knew that it was more than his job was worth to hum or whistle at 11.59 a.m. even though he could do so with impunity a minute later.

Isaac, who always smiled, also knew that when an ambulance came into view, he was required, if in my father's company, to touch his hair with both hands, a practice which made driving hazardous. It must have been a puzzling sight to passing motorists to behold all the occupants of the Stock vehicle touching their respective heads as an ambulance shot by. You might well ask after the rationale for this habit though rationality and superstition are contradictions in terms.

Well, it goes like this: touching hair was the physical expression of the sentiment, 'Touch hair, never go there'. Get it? If you touched your hair when you saw an ambulance, or when you passed a hospital, you would never go there. Whereas if you didn't touch your hair, there was no question but that within a few minutes thereafter, that is exactly where you'd find yourself. So brainwashed by this practice did I become, that I have observed this tradition even after leaving the parental nest, even to this day, and even when actually *in* an ambulance. More difficult to rationalise was touching hair when passing a cemetery. 'Don't go there for some years yet' would have been understandable. But 'never' was a hope too far.

It's a toss up whether the bewilderment occasioned to passing motorists by the hair touching business exceeded that experienced by passing pedestrians who observed the ritual which followed tripping over or kicking into a paving stone which was not flush with its neighbour. Upon such a mishap, one was required to return forthwith to the offending stone or slab and pass one's foot (the tripping foot) over the protrusion three times, back and forth. That done, one walked on. To pre-empt questions from befuddled members of the public, I would accompany the exercise by a pretence at looking for a lost coin. This is a refinement my father did not deem necessary, for such a ruse mitigated the curative effect of the foot-passing exercise.

It is difficult against this backdrop to say that Dad was a religious man but his religion was, as practised by him, not incongruous with his observance of superstitious rituals. Certainly, Ernest believed that failure to do His will was in itself a recipe for ill fortune.

As typically symptomatic of this, I cite an occasion when, well into my adulthood, a bus ploughed from a side street into my vehicle on a Friday evening. I remember it well. It was in Hong Kong and I had taken the trouble to drive my parents to the New Territories, there to show them the sights. The showing of the sights took longer than had been planned, so that at the time we might otherwise have been in synagogue to welcome the Sabbath, we were travelling down the main street of Fanling. Suddenly, from out of a side street and paying too little regard to a 'Give Way' sign, came a minibus which clipped the rear nearside wing of our vehicle. Now, I'm not one to attribute blame where blame is not due, but there was no question in this instance as to where the fault lay. Indeed, so obvious was it that the fault lay with the bus driver that the man emerged sufficiently chastened as to apologise profusely before I even had time to assert that he was liable for the accident. But as far as Dad was concerned, the fault lay not with the bus driver. His liability was irrelevant. It was not to the point. The point was that I had so arranged events as to miss the synagogue service and therein lay the cause of the mishap.

"I told you." (He had told me nothing actually but never mind.) "I told you," he said, square jawed, teeth grinding. "This is what comes from not going to shul."

The Lord, amidst a myriad of commitments that day in all corners of a war-torn, disease-ridden-world, had apparently decided that, as my punishment for not getting us all to synagogue on the Sabbath eve, He would cause a minibus driver in Hong Kong to glance at his fingernails whilst approaching a Give Way sign and steer recklessly into my relatively new Datsun. I should have known.

Sometimes there was less of a causal connection, by which I mean that sometimes the predilection to blame others came to the fore with no superstition in play. One of my cousins, Herbert, the son of Dad's sister, Selma, came to Rhodesia as a youngster. In the early years of his African adventure, Dad suffered a serious horse-riding accident. The horse shied when coming across a snake in the bush and Dad was thrown partially from the mount but dragged along with a foot still in a stirrup. He spent three months in hospital and on his discharge had, on the particular day in question, to travel to a remote location to inspect a herd of cattle. He was too incapacitated to drive. So Herbert was cajoled to arise at 4 a.m. to drive Dad 120 miles to his intended destination on bumpy dirt and mud tracks, to stand with him upon arrival in the heat of the sub-tropical sun while Dad inspected the animals and to drive him 120 dusty miles back again.

Herbert was only fourteen at the time, which, given the fact that there was business to be done, bothered no one. How confident one might feel with so young a driver over such a distance in rough conditions was irrelevant. What is relevant is that when they arrived, there was an ox missing, none too surprising given the large numbers involved and the wide area in which they roamed. But that too was not relevant. The point was that the misfortune had to find a cause. The cause was not difficult to identify. So far as the eye could tell, there were only two human souls within a 100 mile radius and one of them was my father. Well, he was obviously not to blame. So who else but Herbert was there? Quod est demonstratum. A single irresistible inference. Naturally, Dad rounded on him, this 14-year-old early-rising do-gooder, and volubly informed him with resonance, rage, and utter conviction that had he only not brought Herbert along, the bloody ox would not be missing. Voila.

Dad laid tefillin, that is, he donned phylacteries each morning, save on the Sabbath and on High Holydays. Nothing would detract him from this observance, especially on vacation when we were anxious to go to the beach. As it is written: 'You shall bind them as a sign upon your hand and they shall be for a reminder between your eyes.' And that is what he did, wrapped each morning in a prayer shawl, siddur in hand, sitting on the edge of his bed, and whispering the prayers to himself and the Lord. This is where he felt at home, at peace, wrapped in his faith and his heritage, a heritage of great antiquity.

My mother had no superstitions. Save one. It manifested itself in the need to convey negative news in a whisper. If someone was seriously ill, it was not possible to ascertain from her the cause, no matter how well-informed was she, for the cause was spoken in such a hush that one was left none the wiser. One was left to interpret the shape of the mouth, whether it was a 'C' for cancer or, more specifically a 'leu' for leukemia. It tended to be one or the other.

There was another trait which few guessed. She was a giggler. This quiet, highly dignified lady, smart, well-dressed, hair tied tightly, was wont to dissolve in an instant to giggling paralysis at piano concerts, all of which were staged in the Bulawayo City Hall, famed for its awful acoustics; she and I listening to an aged Polish pianist who stopped every few bars to blow his nose with his handkerchief, Mother stopping every few bars with her handkerchief too, stuffed in her mouth.

In due course Herbert, the 14-year-old driver, became Herbert the family man, unaffected, it seemed, by the incident of the missing ox. He died many years later, suddenly, of a heart attack whilst watching a rugby match in Johannesburg. He was jocular. His mother, Selma, was his antithesis for she can best be described as a sigh which is why she had a vast bosom: to retain sufficient lung capacity at any given moment for the length of her prolonged sighs.

As prolonged as Herbert's farts. I wish I could remember Herbert for something else, truly. But I remember him not exactly for his farts but for the manner in which he heralded their production – by the extension of the forefinger of his right hand plus a request to whomsoever was standing closest to pull the finger, a request which, amazingly, was never rejected, so politely was it conveyed. And the pulling effected the fart. No pulling, no fart. Maybe the incident of the missing ox left its mark after all.

Chapter Nine

My birth certificate tells me that I was born in the colony of Southern Rhodesia. The copy of the certificate which I possess is dated October 1946 and has affixed to it a postage stamp bearing the sum five shillings and a picture of King George VI. The same document has a space for 'Race' and mine is described as 'European'. The word 'Caucasian' seems not then to have been in vogue and I suppose it was thought necessary to stipulate race for the benefit of the colourblind who but for the description might have assumed one was not what one was. Heaven forbid. Be that as it may, I was not only European but also a British subject which was not quite as smart as being a British citizen.

We sang 'God Save the King' and after February 1952 'God Save the Queen'. These anthems were played in the cinema before the commencement of each film. The anthem which came to be adopted as that of the pan-African liberation struggle – 'Nkosi Sikelel'iAfrika' ('Lord Bless Africa') – wasn't an anthem we had heard or, if we had, we did not sing it. Only much later did its stirring cry convey to the outsider who cared to listen, the powerful message that the African heart yearned to exercise sovereignty over its own land.

We called the cinema 'the bioscope' although the definite article was omitted, as in "I'm going to bioscope." So in the cinema, we would stand with hands to our sides when the anthem was played and there was the young queen, with a hint of a smile, sitting astride a horse, side saddle, I think; a black horse I seem to recall, all in monochrome with a Union Jack fluttering patriotically in the background.

Then we would sit and someone would walk down the aisle selling penny cools. A penny cool was a plastic container, much like a condom, which housed flavoured liquid, and the trick was to bite off one end without spilling the contents on one's shorts. Shorts, not longs, for no self-respecting male youth wore longs, except on his bar mitzvah or in winter at school. When shorts were donned, they were worn with long socks – long, as in-calf length with the top folded down once and held up with a garter or piece of wide elastic hidden under the folded down bit. Some, only a few, wore short socks and sandals but they were the newly-arrived Poms and they soon conformed.

Bioscope, when one was not yet a teenager of courting years, was visited upon a Saturday afternoon to see cowboy films. Saturday morning was synagogue time, to pray for the well-being of mankind, though preferably of Jews. Saturday afternoon was for witnessing mankind practising killing, with white cowboys killing red Indians or bank robbers. Political correctness had not yet struck the consciousness of the West, let alone white Africa, so there was no notion of referring to the chap in the wigwam as a Native American.

This weekly fest was enjoyed at the Palace Cinema, one of two or three cinema houses in town. The Palace was a large white two-storey construction in art-deco style, with substantial white pillars adorning the frontage. The building still stands although it is now used as a church, no doubt in penance for the multitudes shot by the cowboys.

In later years, bioscope fulfilled two other purposes.

The first was cigarettes. There was no such thing as smoking in the presence of adults, and no such thing as admitting to any adult that one smoked. This was all before the days when the health hazards of smoking were known, though I am not sure that that would have made any difference.

How we afforded to buy cigarettes, I don't recall, though in the tobacco growing country which was Rhodesia, cigarettes – even cigarettes of quality – were cheap. They came in oblong yellow packets of thirty and I favoured a brand called Matinee. I must have started before I was fifteen because I moved from Fife Street then and can still see myself lighting up a fag in the sanitary lane behind the Fife Street house and then seeking to avoid detection until after I had locked the bathroom door to brush my teeth.

So a visit to the cinema was an occasion for lighting up. Smoking in public places was permitted. No one had yet thought that it was anti-social and the notion of secondary inhalation had not yet come about.

The other reason for going to the bioscope was to sit next to a girlfriend. Or to sit next to a girl whom one hoped would be sufficiently fooled by the dim lighting into finding one attractive enough to become one's girlfriend.

Or, if all went really well, to hold her hand and steal a kiss, preferably a prolonged episode of some passion which the dark surroundings and the back row location would hide from the view of those who went to the movies to watch the movie.

These episodes required patience and determination, which didn't always meet with success.

The first step was to hold a hand. This could take a while but it was a vital hurdle. Failure to achieve hand-holding was a certain signal that a kiss was out of the question.

Concentration was imperative; the film was irrelevant. Much energy was expended on finding novel excuses to sit close, touch shoulders, then the side of her hand, then to hold it. This might take all of half an hour but was thought to be well worth the effort. Failure was signalled by a sudden dig in the ribs, or a firm and determined replacing of the male hand on his side of the seat divider; this was interpreted as a wasted afternoon and tended to effect a desire to leave before the movie was half-way through. Or perhaps to light a cigarette in consolation.

But failure, when it occurred, made no difference to the tale that was told at school the next Monday. Every Monday morning was replete with tales of success, some true, most imagined and others rejected as unlikely because of the prior failure of others with the same lass or the lad's reputation for halitosis.

The first film I ever saw was 'Red Shoes' starring Moira Shearer. All I recall is that it was about a dancer who is propelled by these shoes to dance herself under a train, thereby suffering fatal wounds which explains why her fans, eagerly waiting for curtain up on her next performance are told that she is unfortunately indisposed. There is no promise of a refund. That was long, long before the dating years were upon me.

Other titles which made an impression on me were 'Where No Vultures Fly', 'The Man in the Gray Flannel Suit', 'My Pal Gus' and 'King Solomon's Mines'. 'Where No Vultures Fly' was about ivory poaching (*plus sa change*) and 'The Man in the Gray Flannel Suit' starring Gregory Peck was about a married man who has accidentally killed his best friend and has impregnated a girlfriend back in Italy, no doubt also accidentally. Gus in 'My Pal Gus' was the son over whom there raged a custody battle, with his dad falling in love with his teacher, a forgivable enough happenstance, a film I now see described as a comedy drama but I recall nothing funny about it; and in 'King Solomon's Mines' yet another American falls in love with a woman who is looking not only for a mine but for her husband who may, for all the audience cared, have fallen down it.

The main feature was often preceded by a short film, maybe a cartoon, and by the Pathe News, which in turn was preceded by advertisements, though of a variety somewhat less image-centric than the present garbage.

These adverts frequently included one by Henock Ranching, offering to sell horses. This was of personal interest to me because Henock Ranching was the family company.

'Henock' was a conflation of the names 'Henry' and 'Stock', which put my nose out of joint somewhat because I was so obviously excluded. There was an attempt to befool me with the explanation that the 'n' in 'Henock' represented the 'n' in 'Frank', a suggestion which I found less than convincing. So, to assuage my wounded pride, my father formed another company called 'Frasto Farms'.

I remained sceptical and inquired what aspect of the farming, cattle dealing, animal breeding, horse and mule trading, crop growing business was represented by this new corporate vehicle and discovered that it was created to cater for all aspects of the business that didn't involve farming, cattle dealing, animal breeding, horse and mule trading and crop growing. Frasto Farms did nothing. It didn't even grow grass. It existed as a sop to my pride and for all I know is still on the books.

Chapter Ten

The reader will be under the impression that eisteddfods are competitive festivals of music and poetry in Wales. The Welsh nation and the Concise Oxford English Dictionary certainly say so and I have been to Llangollen to the real thing. Yet I have also taken part, not in Llangollen, but in Bulawayo. We had eisteddfods in Rhodesia. It was part of keeping up with the arts, and calling these art performance competitions 'eisteddfods' was part of keeping us British.

With annual regularity, we celebrated Empire Day. Whether the indigenous population celebrated as well was not a question we asked of ourselves. It wasn't a public holiday but an event nonetheless, marked by special anthems at school, such as Parry's 'Jerusalem' in which the question is asked whether it might be that 'those feet in ancient times walked upon England's green and pleasant land', though there is little evidence to suppose that they had.

Allusion to Empire and royalty was everywhere to be found, even in the 'Authorised Daily Prayer Book of the United Hebrew Congregation of the British Empire', a book which was said to have been 'revised under the direction of the late Dr Hertz, Chief Rabbi'; a posthumous feat entrusted only to Chief Rabbis. It was printed by Eyre and Spottiswoode Ltd 'Her Majesty's Printers'. Extraordinary, what with coronations and garden party invitations, that they had time for the Hebrew Prayer Book. And in the course of every sabbath morning service, between reading a portion of the Torah and the saying of the Amidah, there was intoned a prayer for the Royal Family, seeking heavenly blessing for 'Our Sovereign Lady, Queen Elizabeth; Elizabeth the Queen Mother; Philip Duke of Edinburgh; Charles Duke of Cornwall (as he then was) and all the Royal family.' And, so as to ward off the evil eye, and for good measure, there was also thrown in a prayer for the welfare of the colonial government of the country, that they may 'deal justly and truly with all Israel'; an exhortation still articulated to this day in synagogues around the world with suitable adaptations to local conditions, a prayer which has been answered with mixed success.

Yet we were loyal to the royals. My mother recounted how, when she arrived in the country and first heard the singing of 'God Save the King', she wept, for it signified to her a dignity and fundamental decency which was the antithesis of all that was represented by 'Deutschland Uber Alles', the sound of which, if truth be told, makes me shudder to this day.

The truth is also that I often wished when that prayer for the royals was read in synagogue that non-Jews would hear it, a wish born of a shameful desire for approval, for being seen as something other than alien corn. The victory of the Eastern Jew over the German Jew, so it seems to me, is that the former cared not what 'they' thought of him. It was a lesson which bitter experience moved my parents to impress upon me the fact that no matter how I might seek to hide my racial, national, genetic identity – call it what you will – in order to secure acceptance, I would never succeed. 'They' would know; and I would know that they knew and the very fact of acceptance, when it was conferred, was a concession and a concession is of itself arrogance in the donor and demeaning of the recipient.

And my parents were right. It was proved each time I overheard an anti-Semitic remark and the sense of belonging to a distinct tribe – often a comforting sense – was evident each time I passed a synagogue or entered the company of fellow Jews and each time Israel went to war. And at last, late in life, when I went to Israel, I found myself in a country where a Jew had to prove himself to no one. And that was an intensely good feeling. I was in a country which, save once, I had never before visited and yet I was immediately at home, amongst my people; a mix of all nationalities and colours and the good and the bad and the ugly but there I was judged on the footing of my character and not on the accident of my birth. That the creation of the state of Israel worked significant injustice to those Arabs living there, I do not doubt, yet I find it emotionally impossible to be other than convinced that the establishment of a homeland for the Jews was a necessary answer to centuries of persistent abuse, vilification and murder.

I am reminded by a programme still in my possession that at one eisteddfod there was an adjudicator by name Mr

David Precious who sat next to another named Mrs Sally Strange. Strange and Precious.

In 1954, the admission fee for adults was one shilling, for children, sixpence. The patron of the Eisteddfod Society was Major General Sir John Noble Kennedy, G.C.M.G., K.C.V. O., K.B.E., C.B., and M.C., a list which might be thought to render the name 'Noble' superfluous. Fancy calling a child 'Noble'. Seems to be tempting fate, but I digress.

There is not an African name in the programme. Not one black vice-president, not one black official accompanist, and not one black student competitor. Strange, no? No. Not really. Not then. We just didn't think that way. Except when, as happened each year, some competing choir or other sang 'De Camptown Races' or 'Swing Low, Sweet Chariot' then described as a 'Negro spiritual'.

There was much fervour too. The Bulawayo Presbyterian Church choir sang the grammatically suspect 'He Watching Over Israel'; someone called Doris Thompson rendered an acidic oratorio entitled 'All My Heart Inflamed and Burning'; then a recitative by Acis and Galatea, whoever they may be, sung by one David McHarg, with the title 'I Rage, I Melt, I Burn', followed by Handel's 'O Ruddier Than The Cherry' which, given all the raging, melting and burning, was not surprising. The very same McHarg, who must have been a terrible bore, ended the afternoon with a solo 'Shepherd's, See The Horse's Foaming Mane'. Had our education encouraged Socratic dialogue, some student or other might have asked what a foaming mane was, why the shepherds were asked to behold one and what, having beheld it, they did about it.

My name is there in the programme, under 'Class 115: Speech, Boys, Under 10 Years', two names below the troublesome Watkins and one above Mark Pieters who was famous because his parents, who had no connection with the Antipodes, bore the forenames Sydney and Adelaide.

I was candidate number twenty-four on 1 July 1954. The adjudicator for the performance in question was Ms or Mrs Mathey and the piece entrusted to our recitation was 'Wind's Work', aptly named for its lack of substance and the nervous condition of the young contestants. I still have Ms Mathey's written report which she read out to the gathered declaimers and their parents. I didn't take kindly to what she said. The best she could offer to this nine-year-old whose pronunciation was second to none amongst the juvenile colonial hacks in that neck of Africa was this: "Do not say eh lark. Say u lark. Whistle the 'wh' a little. Drop the hands at the sides. Watch the 'i' vowel. Vowels are quite fair."

Well, I will say now to Mrs Mathey what I wished to say then: "Piss off, Mrs Mathey." And if Mrs Mathey is no longer of this world and has been admitted to the Great Eisteddfod in the Sky, then I say "Piss off" a bit louder, with emphasis on the 'i' of 'piss' and I hope that when she met St Peter at the Pearly Gates, she remembered to drop her hands by her sides and to whistle her 'wh' when she asked "Where can I find a harp?"

Our devotion to Empire evidenced itself in the school curricula; the music we learnt, the hymns we rendered, and the poems we recited. There was no notion in the Southern Rhodesia of the 1950s of an African history before, say, 1893 or thereabouts. In the beginning, God created the heaven and earth and nothing of note happened after that until 1893 when the British South Africa Company entered Rhodesia, as it was not then called, and took defensive action against the ungrateful Matabele. The episode is referred to in a contemporary account edited by Wills and Collingridge as 'The Dawn of Civilisation', a view not shared by the locals or his impis. Thus it was that we learned about the Matabele Rebellion, Cecil Rhodes, Leander Starr Jameson, the Wilson Patrol, Alfred Beit, Frederick Courteney Selous, the Pioneer Column, the British South Africa Police, Clive of India – though not his impeachment trial – and that's about it.

No one thought to ask what was there before 1893 or how and by whom Great Zimbabwe came to be constructed, how Lobengula came to be king, what customs were observed by his followers, what wars they fought and against whom, what caused them to flee the lands of the Zulus, why they chose to migrate as far north as they did or what impact on their personal lives and hearts was wrought by the advent of the British South Africa Company and the planting of its flag in Bulawayo.

In terms of the history we were taught, Africa seemed to matter only in so far as it was British. And white. And, indeed, a substantial proportion of Africa, from Cape to Cairo, was under British administration. In Rhodesia, the capital was called Salisbury, there was a fort called Fort Victoria, and the thunderous magnificent falls were named Victoria Falls. In Northern Rhodesia, African names made way for Livingstone, Fort Jameson, Fort Rosebery and Abercorn.

The piano examinations to which I was subjected were set by the Associated Board of the Royal School of Music and they sent examiners from the Mother country to test us on pieces by English composers of whom none in the real music world had ever heard. So, for example, we plonked a piece by a chap called Eric H Thiman which he entitled 'Hop on my

Thumb', the only piece it seems he ever composed, perhaps because someone took him at his word.

On one Speech Night alone, years later, the school choir sang 'Greensleeves', 'O Peaceful England', 'The New Commonwealth' by Vaughan Williams, 'Admirals All' by Newbolt, 'Jerusalem' of course and, in case anyone had lost the theme, Sir Hubert Parry's 'England'.

My burgeoning thespian talents were accorded an airing that night by a rendition of the speech by Elizabeth I at Tilbury Docks, which took some courage on my part, I can tell you, at the moment when I declared in the presence of approximately 1300 school boys that, although sporting the heart and stomach of a king, "I know I have the body of a weak and feeble woman."

And in attendance was the Rt Hon the Earl of Dalhousie, Governor General of the doomed Federation of Rhodesia and Nyasaland. God Save the Queen. God Save Dalhousie. And God Save Me.

There were also public speaking competitions run by the Royal Commonwealth Society – Bulawayo Branch. One such was staged in the Beit Hall of our school with some evidence of a relaxation of racial preponderances, for taking part were not only the usual 'white' schools – Eveline High, Townsend High, Hamilton High, Founders High, St Peters, and Milton High but also the Luveve Technical College, a college attended only by blacks.

The subject matters were predictably Commonwealth oriented – the British Commonwealth, for there was none other: 'Describe four interesting places in the Commonwealth that you would like to visit'; 'Compare living conditions in two widely separated Commonwealth Countries'; and 'Is the

Westminster pattern of government suitable for emergent Commonwealth nations?'

I was allotted the last of these subjects and was criticised by the adjudicators on two grounds: first, that I seemed not to appreciate that there were Commonwealth countries outside Africa and second that there was a certain 'affectation' about my presentation. Be that as it may, I reached the finals which were staged before an audience of appreciative parents as well as before His Excellency Sir Humphrey Gibbs, Governor of Southern Rhodesia.

History does not record the meat of my presentation though it is unlikely that I would have suggested that the Westminster pattern was anything other than ideal. History does however suggest, thus far at least, that the Westminster pattern has not been embraced by Commonwealth countries with universal enthusiasm or success.

To underscore the strong connection with the Mother country, compliant royals were from time to time rolled out for visits to the Empire. The king visited in 1947 but I was too young then to remember and, as far as I'm aware, neither he nor any member of his family came to our apartment in Grey Street. Mr Adams, whose leg was in plaster, who did come, was not a member of the royal family.

I was eight when the Queen Mother and Princess Margaret descended upon Bulawayo in 1953 to officiate at the opening of the Rhodes Centenary Exhibition. It was called the Centenary Exhibition because it took place one hundred years after Cecil's birth. No one now celebrates Cecil's existence let alone his birth, but it was a big deal then; after all, the country bore his name.

An extensive piece of land was set aside in Bulawayo to

house the exhibitions in pavilions representing numerous countries, an area maintained as the Centenary Park for years thereafter. The Queen Mother and her younger daughter were greeted by the then prime minister, one Godfrey Huggins and about two thousand people in the Queen's Grounds. Distinguished artists came from the UK to perform in the substantial theatre designed and erected for the festival, appropriately named the Theatre Royal. Amongst the performers were John Gielgud and George Formby, though the two did not appear in the same production. There was ballet, I remember – it didn't appeal to me – and the Halle Orchestra was conducted by Sir John Barbirolli. I was impressed not so much by the orchestra or its music or by the conductor's expertise as I was by the fact that an Italian had become a Knight of the Realm. That fact alone provided me with an incentive to become a world famous conductor and I would stand in my parents' lounge (when they were not at home) vigorously conducting imaginary orchestras, but soon decided that the exertion required was not worth it unless a knighthood could be guaranteed and, being realistic enough to appreciate that there was an element of hit and miss in this prospect, I relinquished the ambition.

Bulawayo had never experienced anything quite as grand as the exhibition and its attendant fanfare and, as far as I am aware, has not experienced the like since. An abiding memory is of the fact that the two royals managed to smile all the while, having to pretend that they were really interested in meeting each and every person to whom, endlessly, they were introduced. The good princess had just been required to end her relationship with Group Captain Townsend, so smiling for her must have been especially difficult. I watched her passing in a motorcade and tried to attract her attention with a nonchalant wave in the hope of making her realise that there were other fish in the sea, but she pretended not to notice me.

Chapter Eleven

When I was aged twelve, I progressed from Milton Junior School to Milton High School. Milton High School, situated at the top of Selborne Avenue and occupying large grounds, was an all-boys school, and an all-white school too. In some ways it was run on (British) public school lines, in its emphasis on sports as a builder of character, its insistence on manners as the measure of character (the school motto was 'Manners Maketh Man'), and in the ready use of corporal punishment for rule infringements.

There was no such thing in those days as sensitivity to academic weakness. So those who were considered academically bright were assigned to the A stream with an order descending to D or even E. The A stream was itself split into 'AL' for those who were to study Latin, and 'AS' for those who were to specialise on the sciences. I found myself in 1AL. It was expected that we would progress through the 'A' stream to the Cambridge School Certificate (the forerunner of the GCSE), and then to the Sixth Form to prepare for university.

There were two dominant sports: rugby and cricket. I excelled at neither. I tried my hand at rugby and so distinguished myself that I was selected to be reserve fly-half for the Under-13 D team. I remember only one game, on the dry dusty patch that was allotted to our lowly level of skill. The rugby master, one Mr McCallum, was kind enough to congratulate me on staying bolt upright in the face of a ferocious tackle, for which the explanation was one of simple physics. Both sides (including my own) conspired by happenstance to come at me with equal and opposite force and, in a clear vindication of Newton's Third Law, I was thus held aloft, clutching the ball, happy not to be on the grit scratching my knees. I wasn't asked to play again.

I did, in later years, excel in table tennis. I played for the school team in the local league and was disappointed when the powers that be at the school declined my suggestion that the sport warranted the award of colours. Those who earned fine reputations at rugby, cricket, and tennis were awarded colours in recognition of their prowess and in consequence were entitled to wear school blazers of light blue instead of dark blue with the name of the relevant sport sewn below the blazer pocket. Perhaps it was thought that the currency would be devalued if some students had labels with the words 'Ping Pong' sewn on their blazers.

But I amused myself both at junior school and later with games of a less strenuous type. Like pencil cricket. Pencil cricket required a six-sided pencil, the edges of which were rendered amenable to ink markings by shaving the paint off each side with a razor and writing in the numbers 1,2,3 ,4 and 6 and the word 'Out' on the respective shaved panels. One then jotted down on a piece of paper the current names of those who played cricket for England and South Africa and thus it was that international games of pencil cricket were played in one's lounge at home or on one's desk in class, with a temptation to cheat if South Africa seemed in danger of losing. In the context of international sporting competitions, South Africa was always stronger than Rhodesia and given that fact and that Rhodesia bordered South Africa and the lifestyles were similar, Rhodesians tended to support South African teams; indeed, a number of Rhodesian cricketers and rugby players were selected to play as part of South African national teams. Colin Bland, a Milton School alumnus, became a famous Springbok cricketer and Des van Jaarsvedlt, a Bulawayo boy, was a great Springbok rugby player; though there were others.

More energetic than pencil cricket was table rugby. For this, there was a rubber or, as it is now more safely called since the advent of the condom, an eraser to represent the ball. A line was drawn across and about two inches from each end of the desk and the objective was to flick the eraser along the length of the desk, with such dexterity and finesse as to cause it to halt on the line of one's opponent. That was then a try. If a try was scored, one's opponent was obliged to stand behind his side of the desk with arms, hands and thumbs so configured as to mimic rugby posts. The idea was for the try scorer, from a position in line with the try, to use his forefinger to flick the eraser aloft, over the bar formed by the thumbs and between the posts formed by the forearms. The pleasure of scoring a conversion in this way was enhanced if one could manage to strike the eraser with sufficient force to hit the opponent's face.

Then there was mini-cricket. Mini-cricket was played with a cricket bat the bottom half of which had been sawn off. The stumps were represented either by a wooden crate or the base of a tree. To avoid the possibility of such injury as might be occasioned by a genuine cricket ball, tennis balls were used instead, although it was acceptable to throw a tennis ball directly at the legs of a player, instead of at the stumps, in the hope of bruising him. There were no colours for mini-cricket.

Other games were not connected to forms of recognised sport. One example was bork-bork. This was a dangerous game which risked breaking the backs of the participants. The object was for the lead player of one team to hug the base of a tree with his shoulder and for the other members of his team to hug him in turn so as to form a caterpillar line of bodies, each person bent forward at right angles to the person in front. So far so good. Now comes the dangerous bit. Members of the opposite team then ran one by one and leapt on top of the caterpillar, as far forward as possible and with as much downward force on landing as possible. The object of the exercise was to see how many of the jumping team the bending team could bear before collapsing. There were no colours for bork-bork either.

There was another game the rules for which I can no longer recall. We called it 'kenny kenny' but I have since gathered that in South Africa it is called kennetjie. It involved digging a rut in the dirt a foot or so in length and half an inch deep and placing a short stick across the hole thus formed, flicking that stick aloft with another but longer stick and striking the short stick as far as possible from the rut. The fielder(s) tried to catch the short stick before it landed in which case the 'batsman' was out, failing which a fielder threw the short stick towards the batsman in the hope of striking his leg or landing the short stick in or across the rut. Strange to relate, I was in Burma a few years ago, passing through a nondescript village by the banks of the Irrawaddy River when, lo and behold, I saw a group of village children playing kenny kenny. So it occurred to me as a possibility that the game had been imported to Rhodesia by members of the military who had served in that arena during the Second World War or perhaps by those who had been sent to East Asia in the 1950s to quell the Malaysian uprising. Alternatively, the Rhodesians exported the game to Burma.

And there was Escalado. Escalado required a table long enough to accommodate a green plastic racetrack along which were dotted some small wooden round pegs at regular intervals. The track was made taut by securing the ends with screws over and under the edges of the table, thus ensuring that the dining table, purchased with the hard earned savings of one's dear parents, was forever marked. There were six lead horses, each mounted by a jockey sporting garish racing colours. By means of rotating or cranking a handle attached to the starting end of the track, the horses with their rigid jockeys were jerked forward, each horse faring better or worse than its neighbour according to whether, and if so how often, it stumbled against one of the wooden pegs. These races became more interesting, but the results more predictable, once one or more of the horses contrived to lose a leg.

Attendance at school rugby matches – real rugby matches – was compulsory, at least when the 1st XV were playing. For the schoolboy attendees (as opposed to the players) school uniform had to be worn with boaters, that is to say, straw hats which tastefully displayed school colours.

The highlight of 1st XV rugby matches was the shouting of the school war cry. Prefects would stand facing the schoolboys in front of the touchline and shout and the schoolboys were required to shout back. The Milton School war cry was rather lacking in poetic imagination or in the terror it was likely to induce in the opposition, certainly by comparison with the All Blacks hakka. It went like this, I kid you not:

Prefects (taking off their boaters and thrusting them downwards): "GuBulawayo!"

School (in a low bass descending groan): "Eeeee!"

Prefects: "GuBulawayo!"

School: "Eeeee!"

All (at heightened pace): "Enok. Enok. Enok. Ayyy." (Short breath). "Enok. Enok. Enok. Ayyy. MILTON!"

I have no idea who Enok was or why his name, if it was a name, had to be repeated so often but no one ever inquired. Perhaps he was the groundsman and this was our way of thanking him for keeping the field in a suitably dangerous condition.

Anyway, the games were eagerly fought with such opponents as Falcon College, Plumtree School, and Peterhouse. Results were announced in the school hall on the following Monday at assembly and greeted with applause, regardless of the particular outcome. There was no announcement of the results of the Under 13 D team.

Corporal punishment was meted out liberally by prefects as well as teachers. No one thought it outrageous and there was even an element of heroism in being selected for a caning.

Some canes had names. One teacher named his cane Fifi. Fifi was left on his desk during lessons, always in full sight of the class, *pour encourager les autres*. Another teacher offered the choice of a thrashing forehand or backhand and it fell only to those who didn't know that he was a squash champion to elect backhand.

One teacher was particularly feared. His name was Cowper. By some he was considered a shit. I say 'was' because I think that he's dead. If so, I'll disregard the injunction not to speak ill of the dead by repeating the consensus that he was a shit. He spoke with exaggerated articulation and was nicknamed 'Sludge' on account of his wobbly girth.

I was caned by Sludge. Ah yes, as goes the song from 'Gigi', I remember it well.

I was entering the school gates on foot one morning in the company of a classmate named Michael Goldschmidt. As we were walking in, the headmaster's wife was driving out. In accordance with the courtesy rules of the day, I raised my cap as she passed. Michael did not raise his. He hadn't been paying attention. He planned to become a veterinary surgeon and was probably thinking of a rabbit he was minded to dissect. Sludge was driving in. Sludge stopped his vehicle some fifteen feet or so ahead of us and summoned young Goldschmidt for a dressing down. Quite what possessed me to do it, I don't know, but I shouted out, mimicking Sludge's posh accent, "You bad mannered boy!"

Goldschmidt looked terrified. He clearly thought, with some justification, that I'd taken leave of my senses.

Sludge's bulbous eyes popped out from their sockets and he yelled,: "Boy!" He knew the names of few of us, so 'Boy' was safe.

By this stage, I had reached the driver's window of Sludge's car.

"Were you attempting an imitation of me, boy?" he stupidly asked.

"No, sir," I stupidly lied. "I was attempting to imitate Goldschmidt."

"See me after assembly, boy," he ordered and drove off, leaving me to fret and Goldschmidt off the hook.

I spent assembly unappreciative of the hymn sung that morning, 'To be a Pilgrim' which begins with the words: 'He who would valiant be.'

I duly received a number of strokes on my backside delivered by a cane of sorts. I hold no grudge against Goldschmidt, who indeed lived on to become a veterinary surgeon of considerable renown. My grudge is against Sludge (no rhyme intended). I heard in later years that Sludge became a member of parliament for the Rhodesian Front, the party of Ian Smith, he of the Unilateral Declaration of Independence in 1965. I hope that Sludge sat in parliament with sufficient frequency to develop painful hemorrhoids.

Our teachers were allotted nicknames as is the practice at all schools, even to this day.

Mr McCallum, of rugby Under 13D fame, was named 'Cowboy' for his habit of pretending to draw imaginary pistols on entering the classroom. He taught English and sported a glass eye occasioned, according to legend, by the loss of an eye in a pea shooting mishap. He was known, upon leaving class during a lesson, to ensure the good behaviour of those left behind by removing the eye, placing it on his desk and declaring that he was keeping an eye on us.

Cowboy introduced the word 'doof' into our vocabulary. A doof was a fart. I use the expression to this day though not without thinking, when I do, of Romy Lis, a fellow classmate, whom Cowboy invariably referred to as 'doofer'. Whether Lis, of Jewish Romanian extraction I think, was in fact a doofer I do not know but that is the achievement for which he will forever be fondly remembered by his classmates. Even unto this day.

Our Latin teacher, a Mr Thompson, was allotted the sobriquet 'Vamp' for his vampire features. He had pointed ears in the manner of Mr Spock and slanted eyes and eerie speech to boot, plus a habit of flicking one behind the ears as he walked up and down the aisles formed by the desks, declaiming Latin declensions. "Amo", flick, "amas", flick, "amat", flick. His words of wisdom were few, indeed they were restricted to pointing out, quite correctly yet frequently, that "You get nothing in this life for nothing and very little for sixpence."

Mrs Young was a decent lady who taught economic history, a subject which I found dull but was persuaded to study on the nonsensical advice that if I wished to be a lawyer, I should secure a grasp of economics. Fat lot they knew. For reasons too cruel and impolite to explain, we called her 'Sandbags'.

Englebrecht had no nickname, as far as I recall. But,as his name foretold, he spoke with a strong Afrikaans accent. He taught us geography and he taught the sixth formers economics. He called me 'Stockie'. He knew that my father was a farmer and that as such had access to a ready supply of biltong, a delicacy in that part of the world made of meat dried in strips in the sun. Any butcher shop worth its salt displayed racks of the stuff hanging on hooks. My father went every Saturday after synagogue into town to the Dundee Butchery, run by Mr Heilbron, a German Jew, and went behind the counter to finger the sticks of biltong so as to test whether wet or dry and would order Mr Heilbron to "Give the boy (yours truly) some decent biltong; not some of your rubbish." Heilbron would duly oblige and my father would refuse to pay.

Heilbron and my father fell out with alarming regularity, each – after the latest row and in the privacy of his home – berating the other with a vehemence that increased with the passage of the year. And each year, like clockwork, they made up on the eve of Jewish New Year, as is the custom, with declarations – again in the confines of his home – that the other was in truth a really nice man and what a pity it was that they had fallen out. The New Year reconciliation tended to last a fortnight at most and, save for the Saturday morning visit to Dundee Butchery, the excoriation behind each other's back resumed and lasted for the next eleven months or so.

Englebrecht liked biltong. His opening line on entering class was in the form of a question directed at me: "Stockie, where's my biltong?" He even threatened us with surprise geography tests unless the biltong was forthcoming. But it was all in a jocular vein and I don't think I ever obliged.

We carried biltong in our pockets, to be removed and chewed whenever the fancy took hold, if necessary during class and behind an uplifted desk lid. Either that or gob-stoppers, sweets so called because they were large enough to prevent any air entering one's lungs.

Also smuggled into class, most often under one's shirt, was the occasional bush baby, a creature known for its propensity to stick its head out of the shirt covering and thus ensure confiscation.

Our French teacher was Mr Adlard. He too had no nickname and I remember him as a softly-spoken man whose son Gerald was in our class. Every high school student was required to choose, as an extra language, either French or Afrikaans. Afrikaans is the language of the South African Boer, one of the two official languages of South Africa in those days. Most white students who went on to university chose to do so in South Africa. Therefore many chose Afrikaans, a low Dutch and rather harsh on the ear. I chose French and Mr Adlard.

I do not know why we called 'Guff Guff' by that title and I don't even know his actual name. All I remember is that he walked in a decidedly odd manner, slowly with a marked thrust forward of each leg (in turn of course). It was suggested, as only schoolboys would suggest, that he had some terrible disease. I wish though that I hadn't come across him for I was to pay an embarrassing price in recent years when I entertained my grandchildren with imitations of his walk, telling them that this was how 'Guff Guff' moved. One of them, having misremembered the sobriquet and at an age when she knew not any rude words at all but must at least have overheard this expletive at school, asked me, in the presence of polite company, to demonstrate how Fuck-Fuck walked. How does one explain that to an enraged daughter-in-law?

Chapter Twelve

Rhodesia was a racially divided country. Not in the stark, regimented and legislated manner created by apartheid in South Africa but divided nonetheless with political and economic power garnered by the whites who formed a significant minority of the population.

We mixed socially only with whites. The school populations were all white or all black. Soccer was the sport of the black populace and rugby, cricket, hockey and tennis of the white. I cannot recall during my school years encountering blacks as patrons in restaurants or hotels or cinemas but I do distinctly remember that seating at the circus, a form of entertainment which appealed to the Africans, was divided, and the blacks were consigned to the seating on the sides, the whites in front.

And most whites thought little of it or, if they did, many justified the discrimination on a number of grounds in which they fervently believed: that the black man was uneducated and therefore not ready for political power and would not be ready for the foreseeable future. To boot, he was also lazy, so went the generalisation and if he could steal from you, he would. Sometimes he was even cheeky, would you believe? And what he was really interested in was going to the beer hall on a Sunday afternoon.

That he was uneducated because enough was not spent on his education, that he might steal because he was poor, and that he might resort to drink because there was little else to do were uncomfortable truths, inconvenient to contemplate, let alone acknowledge.

These were the truths as I saw them. Yet in stating them, there is a danger of conveying a distortion of the complete picture and of portraying all whites as harbouring and displaying a contempt for the black population. That would not be true and, unless one is to embark on a studied thesis of the subject, it is difficult fairly to provide a balanced picture which, whilst conveying the indignities suffered by the black man on a day to day basis, at the same time gives voice to the significant section of the white community who did not embrace antipathy or denigration and whose relationship with other races was one of respect.

Societal strata, revealing themselves along racial lines, tended to be justified by those who wished to justify them on the basis that the black man was not ready for political advancement and it is true that the lot of the black man in that part of the world has, since the advent of majority rule, been, in many ways, a bitterly sorry affair, where swathes have, by reason of governmental corruption and mismanagement, been consigned to unemployment, abject poverty and shortened life expectancy. And this is to say nothing – for the world has said nothing of it – of the murder of thousands of black people in Matabeleland by Mugabe's infamous Fifth Brigade in the early 1980s, a brigade trained and equipped by those exemplars of human rights abuses, the North Korean authorities. And yet, none of this answers the affront to human dignity which was a fact of life, at least as I perceived it and, since this is a personal memoir and not a political treatise, I must recount the injustices as they appeared to me when I lived there and to identify the essence of that perceived injustice.

I can't say at what precise point my consciousness of the injustice was aroused or heightened. It was no doubt a cumulative process. It may have been the drip drip of the manner in which employees were castigated; the fact of white children – not all, but enough – speaking condescendingly to a black adult; or the thrashing I once saw a white employer administer to his black employee with no fear of retribution or prosecution; or my witnessing, on more than one occasion, a black man seeking charity or a job from a white man being told, dismissively and cruelly, I thought, to go instead and ask Joshua Nkomo for a handout or a job.

But if I am to choose an incident from all others, I would choose the incident I witnessed in the sanitary lane close to our house in Fife Street, an incident which I can see before me today as clearly as then.

I was walking – of an afternoon, I think – from my house in Fife Street to Nehemiah's house a block away, or maybe it was to the synagogue, on the dusty pavement past the sanitary lane running from 3rd Avenue to 4th, when I saw in the lane a young white lad, aged ten perhaps, throwing stones at a black man, an adult. Whether the adult ventured some form of verbal protest, I can't now recall. But I can say that there was no threat of reporting to the boy's parents and no possibility of any meaningful recourse. This was not, in my experience, a common occurrence but the occurrence and the roles of the two individuals encapsulated at once the evil represented by attitudes of racial superiority and that evil is the denial of the dignity of the individual, the stripping of his self-respect. That is what the societal dispensation bred. The boy thought it permissible to act as he did and the man lived in a milieu in which such things happened and he was expected to put up with it.

It was the affront to dignity which triggered my sense of outrage; his powerlessness to assert himself as a man, his relegation to passivity, the exposure of his low societal ranking, the stripping of his worth as a fellow being or, to put it more accurately, the failure to recognise that he possessed or was entitled, as a matter of fundamental decency, inherent dignity at all. And it is that right, the right to one's dignity, that has consequently embedded itself in my conscience as the core right from which all other rights flow. In the sense that each individual has a different talent, that each contributes differently and with varying effect to society, we are not equal; yet are we not all equal in the respectful consideration to which at the outset we are entitled? We may lose that entitlement or a degree of it through the choices which we freely make in the course of our lives but the circumstance of our birth is not a choice we make: that much is self-evidently true and since it is self-evidently true and admits of no qualification, it follows that a denial of respect and the consequential denigration of inherent dignity, based, not on our conduct, but on circumstances outside of our individual control is a denial which is searingly unjust, uncivilised and cruel.

As to the beating to which I have referred, it was administered by a white adult in a backyard not far from our home, upon a black employee for neglecting his duty, accompanied by shouting at him that he was a bastard. And whilst he was thus delivering this punishment, other employees were present as was a white child of the employer. I knew the white family and I was surprised because they were generally of kindly disposition and the employer had obviously lost his temper and was probably acting out of character. But it was an incident that deeply offended my innate sense of what was just, illustrative of the powerlessness of the black man.

Only once did I see a black man strike back and it was a fight indeed. I do not recall how it started but it took place one afternoon outside the Hebrew School and the combatants were of similar age – in their late teens or early twenties and each of strong build. I have no idea now who hit who first but it was an equal battle and, as far as I am aware, carried no consequences after the fight.

Our domestic employees lived in 'servants' quarters dwarfed in size and levels of comfort by the households they served. Whites were called 'Master' and 'Madam' by men who were called 'boys'. Even white youths were called 'Master' by adult black domestic employees. The criminal courts, in which the vast majority of defendants were black, were administered exclusively by whites, with white judges and white advocates and white assessors, all speaking a white man's language. Pay disparities were vast and power, both political and economic, lay in the hands of a small minority who intended to keep it that way. Land and natural resources were not allocated on an equitable basis, a point made by Sir Robert Tredgold in his instructive 1968 autobiography 'The Rhodesia that was My Life'. Sir Robert was a distinguished public servant who became Chief Justice of the Federation of Rhodesia and Nyasaland. He points out that approximately the same area had been assigned to two hundred thousand or so whites as to four million blacks. And for the black man, there was no amelioration in sight, no hope of an escape from a subservience to which he was consigned by an accident of birth. He had scant representation in parliament and the legislative vehicle for change, if change was to come, lay in the hands of those who either wanted no change at all or were, in some cases, prepared to concede change at a pace which was slow.

It is perhaps odd and patronising to observe, since it can rightly be said to be an assertion of what should be expected in any event, that many white employers treated their domestic helpers or farm hands or factory workers well, often employing them until old age and being solicitous of the welfare of their families. The observation is offered not to suggest that this fundamental decency, when practiced, merits special praise but rather because it is part of the condition which in fact prevailed. Most farmers and their children spoke the local African dialect and ensured that their employees received proper medical attention and some close friendships developed between the children of farmers and the children of farm workers. On Dad's farm, for instance, there was a man named Gideon, a first class horseman, employed by my father for many years and engaged to show horses off to their best vantage when buyers came to the farm. Henry and he developed a friendship born of mutual respect mixed with a shared sense of humour. Even so, there was no question of mixing at the social level. Their worlds were different and, when push came to shove, one world was a world of privilege, the other of subservience.

It is no answer, so it seems to me, to the injustices of which I speak to say that the subsequent history of the African continent illustrates an unreadiness for responsible government, responsible in the sense of sound economic management and respect for the rule of law. The powerful retort to that argument – an argument so frequently deployed to this day – was provided in a Facebook contribution I recently read by an African in response to a suggestion by a white man that the African of today would rather the return of white colonial rule, so poor has his lot become under post-colonial rule. No, he replied, if given the choice between the relative economic advancement that such a reversion may bring and on the other hand to have his mother, a domestic helper, provided with left-overs from the white table and spoken to as if she were a dog (his words, not mine), it is his mother's dignity which he would choose. The thorough mess that is today's Africa is not a justification for the daily affronts to the dignity of the black man in colonial times.

It should have come as no surprise that by the late 1950s, there commenced the breeze which was to develop into the wind of change. In 1960 there were riots in Bulawayo, at a time when the country was part of a political federation of Southern Rhodesia, Northern Rhodesia and Nyasaland, with

Roy Welensky as its prime minister and Joshua Nkomo the leader of African nationalism in the South.

To a white schoolboy, it was all quite exciting, with parents glued to the radio news and photographs in the Bulawayo Chronicle of troops in armoured carriers patrolling The Location.

And in April 1959, there was a debate in Form 2A1, in which I took part, but which did not make the national news. According to my notebook of the time, the motion before the house was: 'The Press Should be Free without any Restrictions.' Whatever my private views might have been, I, then aged thirteen, was assigned to oppose the motion and it seems that I had no compunction in saying that if indeed the press were free to say whatever it wished, people would 'be scared to look at a newspaper'.

So far, that was a rather immature and unrealistic statement but not racist. Yet the very next suggestion in my notes, recorded in fountain pen blue ink, was that '.. during the recent crisis in the Federation, it would have been much better if the newspapers had not told everybody so much. And many Africans too were literate' and might be spurred on by what they read. Heaven forbid. My present embarrassment at having written that garbage is mitigated only by the fact that I wrote after the event, in the same notebook, that the proposition's argument – the argument contrary to my own – was the better case. Yet my garbage is what we felt free to say. It reflected a common point of view, that it didn't do to educate the black man too much. He might, in the vein of language used in the American Deep South, become an uppity black.

Against this background of troubles on the horizon, military conscription of all white males, upon leaving school or university, was taken for granted. But military training started well before then. Upon entering high school, all white boys were required to enter the cadet corps.

Chapter Thirteen

Cadets had two facets – the theory and the practice. The theory was taught in the classroom, leading to the writing of the Cert A exams. It consisted of learning to read maps, to know signals, and to understand field craft. This I preferred to the practice, for it required no more than sitting on one's backside, and passing written tests.

The practical side was another story. Broadly speaking, it was drill and rifle skills. At this I was poor. That I was not an enthusiast goes without saying. But it's difficult to exaggerate the degree to which I was no good at drill and rifle handling and shooting.

Each Friday afternoon, we were required, from the age of thirteen, to don our khaki uniforms. Khaki shirt, khaki shorts, heavy black boots with knee-length socks and puttees, belts with brass buckles, and bush type hats with leather chin straps. The shirts and shorts were starched and required to be ironed with neat creases, the boots to be shined and the brass to be buffed to perfection. This spotlessness was the least of my worries since our house servant had himself been in the army (they took selected African volunteers) and was adept in attending to my kit.

Each session we were given a rifle. I was skinny and the rifle, kept at a slope on my shoulder, dug into my left clavicle.

Thus clad, we were dragooned into platoons and senior boys, accorded cadet officer ranks, and school masters trained us and bellowed orders.

Up and down they made us march on the tarred area outside the sixth form buildings. Left right, left right, squad halt, about turn, stand at ease, attention, stand easy, slow march, by the left quick march, slope arms, shoulder arms, present arms.

There was always the idiot who couldn't move his arms in opposition to the corresponding leg. It was one flaw I didn't share.

I started my career as a cadet with a significant disadvantage. Henry had been in the cadets before me. He had been a sergeant major. He enjoyed cadets. He enjoyed being the sergeant major. And in that capacity, he shouted at others, and no doubt on occasion made them run with rifle held aloft as standard punishment for an infringement. Or perhaps he made them keep wet a slab of paving with the aid of only a tooth brush and a cup of water. Stuff like that.

Now, by the time I became a cadet, those at whom he had shouted and those whom he had made run up and down and keep paving stones wet with toothbrushes, were no longer at the rank of private. They were themselves the officers or the sergeants. They were the shouters and the instruments of discipline. And you can see where this is heading.

As soon as they heard my name and had received from me confirmation that my brother was the Henry Stock who had regularly shat on them in years of yore, I was a marked man; doomed. The injustice of exacting retribution by proxy was irrelevant. It was the only retribution to be had. And so it was that I became adept at wetting slabs with a toothbrush (a different toothbrush each week) and, more painfully, running around a courtyard with a rifle over my head, an exercise which made sure I remained skinny.

Never was the lamentable character of my military skills so sorely revealed as when we went each year for a week to army camp, at Llewellyn Barracks, outside Bulawayo. Llewellyn Barracks was the, or one of the, country's main army depots. We were sent there every year to acquire a taste, a mere morsel, of the real thing.

I still possess a list in my own manuscript of items required for one such camp. I was required to take one pair of underwear as well as a change of underwear (for one week, that seems barely adequate), a comb (I had hair then), a pair of 'tackies' (the local patois for plimsolls), a toothbrush, a tin of Blanco (for colouring the army belt), a kit bag (to be drawn from the quartermaster's store), a tin of Duraglit (for polishing brass), boot brush and polish (for making the boots so shiny that one could see one's face in them), and my Cert A badge (to show that I had passed a theory test).

Our tents were aligned in a neat row and we were instructed how to fold our military mattresses and blankets. The mattresses weren't the inflatable type. Not designed for comfort, the mattress, laughingly so called, was about one quarter of an inch thick and laid on the stony ground. And they had to be in line so that when the tent flaps were open, none of the mattresses and none of the blanket edges was other than exactly flush with all the others. This will come as common place information to anyone who has been near an army camp, but I recall it nonetheless on account of the enormous pride when first the occupants of 'my' tent succeeded; well after the occupants of all the other tents.

My uniform had been ironed to perfection by Norman, our house servant, he of previous army experience. Ironed and starched. But he had contrived to starch the collar so as to create a winged effect, of the type sometimes seen with dinner jacket attire. This was wrong. This was a mistake; whether deliberate or accidental, became irrelevant. This was not how army issue collars were meant to be treated. It went down badly with Serjeant Major Erasmus.

Serjeant Major Erasmus was an Afrikaner, as his name suggested. I had heard of him. He was not a cadet. He was the real thing, a permanent member of the Rhodesian armed forces who was the terror of the regulars. And they let him out on us.

He was the archetypal sergeant major. A rasping voice, with the back of his neck at exactly ninety degrees to the ground, straight from his rigid spine all the way to the top of the rear of a clean shaven head. Flat. A plateau with not even a pimple to disturb the geometric exactitude. And a red face. And a swagger stick. And heavy, heavy boots whose steps one could hear even before he took any. And nicotine stains on his muscular fingers.

I first heard his voice as we were marching, in platoon formation, to the evident amusement of passing regular soldiers. But Erasmus was not amused. He had espied my collars. They were flapping in the breeze.

"Who is that horrible man?" he screamed.

It was an overcast day with thunder in the distance but had the thunder been overhead, his voice would have drowned it.

"Who is that horrible man?"

We wondered, though not aloud, who he could possibly be referring to. I had heard that he was a Jew. This seemed unlikely. His name was certainly not Jewish and his features bore none of the characteristics associated with that tribe, but some said that he had married a Jewess. I hoped then and there that he had, that he had also converted and had, in that context, heard of the injunction against murder, though my hopes were qualified by the knowledge that the Old Testament was full of fire and brimstone, with regular encouragement to death by stoning. It was the New which advocated universal love, and universal love wasn't high on anyone's agenda that afternoon. Still, I harboured the prayer that when he spoke of the dreadful horrible man, he could not mean me.

But he did. He really did. I alone was the horrible man. We were commanded to halt. He stood right behind me, his mouth positioned one-quarter of an inch from the opening to my right ear. If that. His tobacco-tainted breath was close. His voice was as loud as a trumpet. It penetrated my skull, lodged into my brain, and there it resonated as in an echo chamber at full volume.

"You are a horrible man," he thought it necessary to remind me. "A horrible little man. What are you?" he screamed, flipping my winged collars with his swagger stick.

I didn't think it timely to voice the question which occurred to me, whether it was appropriate to use 'a' instead of 'an' before 'horrible' for I knew what was expected of me. I was expected to agree.

So I agreed. "I am a horrible little man."

"Louder!"

I loudly repeated the confession.

"Your shirt is a horrible, horrible shirt!"

"My shirt is a horrible, horrible shirt!"

"And you march as if you have a squib up your arsehole," he informed me. This was clearly a statement of fact and not a suggestion or a question. The question, to which there was only one acceptable answer, followed. "How do you march?"

"I march as if I have a squib up my arsehole, Sergeant!" I dutifully and enthusiastically agreed.

"Louder!"

I shouted it louder, wondering whether the sensation I was beginning to feel in the region of my arsehole was indeed a squib or something more illustrative of the fear I then encountered.

But the real test came with the mock battle. It was a night exercise. In the bush. As in most battles, there were two contesting armies. And as in most battles, the objective was to kill as many of the opposing side as possible, failing which to capture them. How a kill was assessed in a mock battle, short of actually producing a body, which, surprisingly, wasn't encouraged, I don't recall. The capturing part isn't difficult to reconstruct, for I arranged matters so as to be the first captive. The benefit of being the first captive was that one saw out the rest of the night in the relative comfort of the enemy's base.

The trigger for this decision was the mention of snakes. The officer in charge of our group told us, as we descended from the truck that had taken us to our starting point, all the rules, all the dos and don'ts. One of the rules was that under no circumstances were we to remove ourselves from the battle arena and return to our truck, assuming we could find it in the dark. But to this rule there was, he said as an aside, one exception. The exception was if one was bitten by a snake.

Until that moment, this wasn't a possibility which had occurred to me. But the reality of the risk was fortified by the knowledge that we would be spending much of our time on our bellies, crawling, in the dark, in the bush where snakes were to be expected and by his further aside that there were probably loads of snakes about but – as if this made a real difference – few were deadly.

There was no way I was going to risk a snake bite.

Our side split into groups of five. Our particular objective was whispered by the unelected leader of our group, a pointless whisper given that at the moment it was delivered, there was not a soul in sight and we were in the African bush with no human life as far as the eye could see or the ear could hear.

The clouds parted and the moon made its appearance so that visibility improved. We fell flat on to the dust, shifting ourselves forward by our elbows like miniature desert frogs and thus we crawled, presumably in the direction of the enemy. We were going to capture some enemy. I think we possessed rifles with blanks as ammunition. How we managed to crawl with rifles as well, I do not know. But we slithered along, gaining movement inch by inch, and in fact it could have been quite exciting.

Except for snakes. I was worried about snakes.

Suddenly, our group leader motioned us to stop crawling. He pointed to two o'clock. There we could see the silhouettes of the enemy. Some enemy. About ten of them. If they saw us, we would be outnumbered and captured, blindfolded and taken to their base. And that would be that for the night.

Just then, I was sure I heard a slithering movement in the grass. We were in the open with only the grass for cover. We couldn't be seen. I wasn't looking at the enemy. I was looking for the snake.

We lay on our stomachs, with the smell of the African earth in our nostrils. I was last in the line. Slowly, ever so slowly, my backside rose into view. What propelled it to do so, I refuse to say. I will assert that it was beyond my control. Some neuron in my brain sent a quiet but unqualified signal to my bum to raise itself above the line of the grass.

So, as bad luck would have it, one of the enemy saw my buttocks inconsistent with the lie of the veld.

We put up a brave fight and one of our number made off on his own into the night but four of us were captured, our arms twisted behind our backs and we were frogmarched to the enemy camp. The march took a mere twenty minutes or so. The battle had barely commenced. It transpired that we were the first captives of the night and there remained about eight hours before dawn and the end of the campaign.

The enemy camp comprised a clearing amongst an array of thorn trees and we were put under the charge of half a dozen or so guards. We were made to sit on the hard earth. There was a small fire in the middle of the camp. An officer came and took our names, to record the fact of our capture which constituted points in our enemy's favour. He congratulated our captors and wondered out loud how we had managed to succumb so early in the piece.

I relaxed. The war was over. We spoke quietly and speculated as to how it was that our presence had been discovered, given that we had all been astute to lie very flat and quiet. It was a mystery.

Then came a development which I hadn't expected. One of our number, a lad called Millar, a square-jawed boy with mustard-coloured curly hair, suggested that we escape.

This was madness. Here we were in the relative bush comfort of stress-free captivity, with a fire to ward off any reptile within half a mile, and Millar wanted to return to the wild and crawl on his belly again.

I suggested that we put the matter to a vote but I was ignored. I then ventured the liberal idea that whomsoever amongst us wished to escape should be free to make the attempt but that he who thought it a bad idea should be free to stay behind. I was ignored again and so we escaped, our captors having let down their guard.

We ourselves captured none that night and roamed about the veldt with apparent impunity, to return in due course to the truck and a welcome mug of hot tea and some Outspan rusks.

My firing skills were a disgrace to any marksman worth his salt. At the firing range, armed with a .303 rifle of Second World War vintage, the shoulder piece of which slammed against the clavicle whenever the trigger was pulled, I seemed adept only at missing the target with such regularity as to provide fodder for the sarcasm of the sergeant major who delighted in suggesting that I be handed over to the enemy since I constituted a danger to the Rhodesian army and its allies.

In the years that followed, army drills and army life took on a life of an altogether more serious consequence for those who remained in the country and who were drawn into combat during the bush wars that followed an indigenous insurgency. Quite a number of them were killed. They fought to maintain a way of life which they viewed as stable and upright and they saw the African struggle as a recipe, were it to succeed, for chaos, corruption and the destruction of Western values. The Africans, on the other hand, saw their struggle as a liberation war, a liberation from political, social and economic oppression, as a fight to regain their land. In truth, it was their land to regain and the way in which they had been held back was not defensible. But the fear that chaos would in due course follow was a fear borne out by events elsewhere in Africa and by the path taken by the country in the late part of the twentieth century and into the twenty-first. Before too long, the country stewed in a cauldron of corruption; in Matabeleland, there took place the premeditated murder of hundreds of men and women by the Mugabe regime and the population of the country as a whole, most particularly the African population itself, was reduced – and remains reduced – to utter poverty and fear.

The Rhodesian soldier was a smart, sturdy and disciplined being, as were the African soldiers on their side whose marching songs can still be heard. But the times, the numbers, and the verdicts of history and of the international community inevitably spelt the end of colonial rule.

Chapter Fourteen

The school year ran from January to December, unlike the school year in the Northern Hemisphere which ran from September until July. Accordingly, our long holidays were spread over six weeks in December and January, which was mid-summer.

The standard get-away for the summer holidays was to South Africa, in our case to Cape Town where a sizable representation of the Stock clan resided, although occasionally we might venture to Durban.

Cape Town is about 1300 miles from Bulawayo and it took a train journey of three days and two nights to travel from one to the other.

The excitement of this train journey cannot be overstated. In the 1950s and 1960s, the trains were pulled by steam locomotives and comprised sleeping cars and a dining car.

Each compartment in each car contained either four or six bunks although at the end of each carriage was a compartment called a coupe which housed only two bunks. If one's family was prepared to pay for comfort, they secured a four bunk compartment, with the upper bunks pushed flush with the walls of the compartment during daytime but pulled out and down at night, with the bedding prepared by a uniformed railway employee. At the window end of the compartment was a hand basin and mirror and at the end of each carriage a toilet. With the aid of a leather strap, wooden slatted blinds were lifted at night to cover the windows so as to shut out the light unless, as was often the case, one preferred to allow in the bright glow of the moon as the flat, sparsely vegetated plains rolled endlessly by to the soporific click-clack of the train's passage along the rails. And the windows could be lowered, a boon when the weather was hot, although it was unwise, as I learned to my cost, to place one's head out of a window lest soot ventured into one's eyes.

Between each carriage was an open space with a guard rail and a narrow connection across which one navigated one's way to the next carriage to see a friend perhaps or, more often, to visit the dining car.

Ah, the dining car to which one was hailed by a waiter promenading back and forth down the corridors of each carriage with an xylophone by which, dressed in a white uniform, he tunelessly announced either the first or second sitting of each meal.

The outside of the carriages were two-tone, a milk chocolate brown on either side of the cream colour which adorned the window surrounds and the words 'Rhodesia Railways' painted in a tasteful yellow on each carriage.

The train journey rocked from Bulawayo through Bechuanaland, now Botswana, stopping at Mafeking, and then, at night, at a one street spot on the map called Mahalapye, a dusty repose of African sleepiness in the middle of nowhere, where we would alight and stretch our legs to a chorus of crickets and other sounds of the hinterland. Then on into South Africa, stopping at railway sidings with only a water tower to mark the location and then onwards, across the Karoo desert to Vryburg and Kimberley and de Aar, through the Hex River mountains and down to the Cape. Rocking, clacking, drumming its long, long way with occasional whistles of the engine.

And at each stop, we examined the wares that peddlars displayed and urged upon the traveler – mostly wood carvings of African animals or lace work – seeking a pittance for their next meal.

On one grand occasion, when I was considered old enough to travel on my own, my father secured for me a coupe for my sole occupation. I knew a few schoolmates on the train and met a girl who was traveling back to South Africa. I must have been about sixteen by then, for my interest in the opposite sex was sufficiently awakened to invite the lass I met to my pad on wheels but I soon discovered that she was somewhat readier than I to explore bodies. I chickened out, she bade me a curt farewell and I spent the remainder of the journey wondering what might have been.

On arrival in Cape Town on that same journey, I had soot in my right eye for I had disobeyed the advice against sticking out my head whilst the train was in motion. Washing the eye with water and trying eye drops failed to dislodge the foreign body so I was taken by my Aunt Emmy to a doctor who tut-tutted at my carelessness, gingerly removed the grit and ordered me to maintain a cotton pad against the eye in question. By the time this minor procedure had finished, my aunt had left the surgery and I was consigned to taking a bus back to Sea Point, where she lived.

Seeing with one eye was more difficult than I had imagined so, on boarding the bus, I took the first seat that appeared available, a seat close to the open entrance to the bus. I wondered why this provoked stares from the people opposite. The bus conductor approached soon after the bus had moved off and he told me that I was required to move to a seat opposite the one I was occupying. I politely declined, telling him that I was fine, thank you. Yet he insisted and I soon discovered why.

It was because I was occupying a seat reserved for non-whites. My padded eye had not seen the sign which designated who was and was not permitted to sit there. The fact that the bus was almost empty and that I was not taking up space desired by any other passenger was altogether irrelevant. I was not a non-white – if you get my double negative – and for that reason alone, I was precluded from sitting where I had sat. Precluded not only by convention but by law. So I moved to the seat opposite and sensitivities and the law were thus sated.

And it occurred to me then how strange it was – not only the law itself but the designation 'non-white'. Whites were not called non-blacks. It was the black who was called non-white, as if white was positive and black was negative. Which, in truth, was how many white men and women perceived it.

These were the days of apartheid in South Africa, where the affront to the individual was all pervasive. It was everywhere. The beaches were segregated, by which I do not mean that the fine beaches were equally divided but that the fine beaches were for whites and the not so fine beaches, out of view of the whites lest they be contaminated by the sight of black people using the same sea, were for blacks and 'coloureds'. 'Coloureds' were people of mixed race. There were public toilets for whites and public toilets for blacks and coloureds. There were park benches for whites and park benches for blacks and coloureds. The hotels were for whites. The cinemas were for whites. The schools were for whites and other schools, in places one did not see, were for blacks and the houses one visited, in which one's relatives resided, were in neighbourhoods where only whites lived, save for their employees who, if they lived on site, did so only with official permission and away from their families.

And all of this was not merely sanctioned by law. It was mandated by law. It was a criminal offence to infringe the directives conveyed by these signs and their designations.

And amongst the laws which were strictly enforced were the immorality laws. They were actually called by that name. There was an Immorality Act which rendered it a serious criminal offence for a person of one race to engage in sexual relations with a member of another. Not just as between whites and blacks but as between whites and 'coloureds' and Asians too. And mixed marriages were prohibited on pain of conviction and imprisonment. Raids were conducted by the police on premises where this immorality was suspected and underclothing seized for proof of the offence, if more direct proof was not available.

Some of those arrested ran as a defence that they were of the same race as the partner with whom they were alleged to have been intimate and to test this, there were methods, reminiscent of Nazi practices, to determine by measurement of features and by hair quality, who was black and who was not.

In support of this way of living, of conducting daily interaction or rather non-interaction amongst the races, of imposing restrictions of movement and the harshest of laws, the whites – or rather, a majority of them – advanced the argument that peoples were different and that these injunctions against mixing were designed to protect natural differences in culture, so that, as the ultimate rationale, it was also to protect the way of life of the non-whites. And the more often they said it, the more they believed it, not stopping to ask how they would feel were the boot on the other foot. Which is strange, given the core teaching of Christianity to do unto others as you would have them do to you. But, even so, some managed to find support in the bible for the societal dispensation which apartheid effected.

If you happened to be born of a mixed union, it was tough. I have heard of a case of a youth who appeared white and was passed off as white but was in fact of mixed birth and when he ventured outdoors, he did so in the company of his white father with his black mother following several steps behind for, out of doors, she played the role of the maid. Only thus could the lad live in the company of both parents.

There was a concession for the Japanese. Japanese people were designated as honorary whites. There was no such thing as an honorary black. Come to think of it, there would have been little point in being an honorary black, since it came with no advantages and a discernible list of drawbacks.

Against this backdrop, it should come as no surprise that the author who made the greatest impression on me was Alan Paton, whose books *Cry the Beloved Country* and *Too Late the Phalarope* bleed the pain of those oppressed by apartheid, a pain born of the fear and humiliation that was the inevitable by-product of the system, a fear that finds its expression in the evocative closing paragraph of *Cry the Beloved Country* which speaks of the dawn which comes each morning to the valley of Umzimkulu and to the township of Ndotsheni, but begs the question, when will come the dawn of emancipation – emancipation from fear and emancipation from bondage?

It was the fear, ever present, which shackled the powerless, a fear created by the machinery of the apartheid regime, a fear which was palpable to anyone who was prepared to see it.

The theme of *Too Late the Phalarope* is the ruination of a white police officer in consequence of a brief relationship with a black woman, thereby contravening the Immorality Act. This swiftly and inexorably brought upon him utter ruination, and his ostracism by close family members and by the white rural community as a whole, guided by their perception of Christian values; a strange recourse, when one thinks about it, since the resulting cruelty and lack of compassion are not Christian values at all. Paton's prose was powerfully poetic and it is an open question whether my inner outrage at racial injustice was triggered by his books or whether the books fed an outrage which was already there.

And so it was that a highlight of the Christmas fayre each year in Cape Town was a carnival called 'the Coon Carnival'.

The 'coons' in this event were the members of the mixed race community who dressed and made themselves up as minstrels, with faces painted black and white and clothes of every imaginable hue and brightly coloured coats and top hats. They danced through the streets singing and playing banjos in troupes which competed against each other for prizes. And each troupe went from hotel garden to hotel garden to display their talents to the guests in the hope of a shilling or two to be deposited in a hat passed around for that purpose. There were no whites or blacks in the Coon Carnival and a standard physical feature of the participants which I remember was the absence of front teeth. This was not arranged for the purpose of the carnival but was – and maybe still is – a cultural phenomenon of those of mixed race in that part of the African Continent.

More often than not, we stayed at the St James Hotel in St James, which is situated on the Indian Ocean side of the Cape peninsula, one of a string of beaches commencing with Muizenberg and ending in Simonstown, then a naval base. So many Rhodesians spent their summer holidays in the Cape that there was a hotel in Simonstown named 'Rhodesia by the Sea'.

Muizenberg was sometimes referred to as 'Jewzenberg' because that was where Jews tended to congregate for their summer holidays, a fact encouraged by the presence of at least one kosher hotel, whose waiters were known for their ability by sleight of hand to produce necessary table cutlery from the grubby pockets of their food-stained jackets.

We set ourselves apart from the crowd who stayed in Muizenberg, perhaps because of a slight snobbishness of which German Jews were accused by those from Eastern Europe. There was some justification in the accusation. The German Jew thought himself a cut above the rest, more cultured, less loud, more assimilated into the ways of the non-Jew, though little good that did them. He dressed in a more refined manner for sure and was, for that reason, known to the Eastern Jew as a *yekke*, the Yiddish word for 'jacket'.

So it was no accident that we stayed at the St James Hotel, a building close to the beach with steps leading up to the hotel from the beach road. The hotel was shaped in a square 'U', painted in white stucco with black timberwork framing the windows and eaves. It was a gentlemanly place, almost an English country inn where children were expected to be observed, if absolutely necessary, but not heard. To the side of the hotel was an extraordinarily long flight of steps up the mountainside, called Jacob's Ladder, clambering up which there were few volunteers from Muizenberg.

The beach was not one of the famous beaches along that stretch of coast; rather it was a pebble beach with a pool built into the sea. So we ate our meals and slept at St James and went to the beach at Muizenberg, a long stretch of white sand with healthy breakers in the relatively warm sea.

Two incidents at the St James Hotel stand out as embedded in Stock history: the incident of the flooding and the case of the deaf mute girlfriend. The two incidents were connected.

I shared a room with Henry. One of us left the bath tap on at night and flooded the room. Henry said I was the culprit. In an attempt to impress the deaf mute girlfriend, I confessed, calculating that being punished would attract her sympathy. But the ruse failed because Henry was blamed as the elder whose responsibility it was to keep an eye on the absent-mindedness of his younger brother.

Ida and Michael Daniel, my maternal grandparents.

Mom and Dad, 1953.

Bela, my cousin, 1940 – 194? (Chapter 4)

Dad, Mom, Henry, and FS on bar mitzvah day.

Bertha and Moses Stock, my paternal grandparents.

Dad and Henry on
the cover of 'The
Rhodesian Farmer'.

Mom in her
twenties.

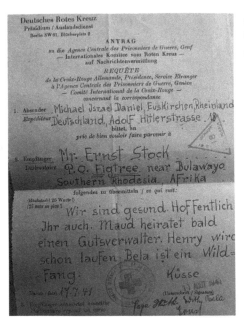

A message through the Red Cross from Mom's parents in Adolf Hitlerstrasse:1941.

Grandfather Michael, WWI.

Class 3A Milton Junior School. Watkins (Chapter 1) front row third from left, FS is fourth from left front row and Nehemiah (Chapter 5) is between them at the back.

The synagogue choir; Cantor Golub in centre front. FS second from right in the next row.

FS in the sixth form

Paul Liptz and FS at university in Salisbury.

Dad receiving the 1000 Guinea Trophy from President Wrathall.

Henry and Frank.

Durban circa 1949

The Stock clan at Henry's bar mitzvah (1953). From L-R: Alfred, Sam, Grete, Helmut, Otto, Emmy, Dad, Henry, Siegfred, Mom, FS, Edna, Lotte, Herbert. Edgar, Selma, Elsa, Heinz.

Edith (Mom's sister) and Mom

This was the first of the hotel flooding incidents for which the Stock brothers were responsible. The other occurred a year or two later at the Langham Hotel in Johannesburg. On that occasion, I ran the bath water and nothing happened. No water emerged from the tap and, not unreasonably, I decided to forgo a bath and went straight to bed. It had not occurred to me to remove the plug or to switch off the tap or that the water might emerge from the unclosed tap with no prior warning and at an inconvenient hour.

I fell into a comfortable sleep, ignorant of the disaster that was lurking in the plumbing. It must have been at about 2 a.m. when I heard the delicate swish swish sound in the room. And the murmuring of men. I wasn't dreaming. Members of the hotel staff had managed to gain entrance to our room – a fact about which it seemed inappropriate to complain, since they were mopping up the water which had over-spilled the sides of the bath which I had only a few hours previously casually abandoned. It transpired that the honeymoon couple in the room below had had their amorous foreplay interrupted by water from the region of the ceiling and they telephoned the hotel telephone exchange, as it was called; one of those arrangements where a row of ladies sits pulling out and shoving in wires and plugs whenever a call was to be made. However, the telephones were not working that evening because some idiot in a room upstairs had left the bath running and the telephone system was 'down'. It was of course all Henry's fault. Again.

I wish I could remember the name of the deaf mute girl but I can see her now. She was pretty, with blonde hair and immaculately dressed, rather, I imagined, like Violet Elizabeth in Richard Compton's books about William Brown, the adventurous English schoolboy. To aid description, let me call her Jane. Jane had an elder sister whose job it was to keep an eye out for her younger and disadvantaged sister.

We met the two girls in the dining room, where talk was small talk and manners were exquisite and our parents struck up a conversation with their parents, who were visitors from England and soon I was playing cards with the girls. I must have been about thirteen or fourteen and Henry was off on his own leading the social life one would expect of a male in his late teens. Jane took a liking to me and I to her. Naturally, conversation between us was somewhat one-sided but still, we hit it off and laughed about nothing in particular.

We went for a drive in her parents' car, her parents in front and Jane, her sister, and I in the back. I was sitting close to Jane. I was holding her hand. Jane's father kept looking in the rear view mirror. I thought him to be an over cautious driver, whereas he was looking with increasing alarm, so I later gathered, at the hand that was not supposed to be touching his daughter's.

We stopped in Simonstown for tea and cakes – scones probably – and the drive back to St James was alive with tension. I signalled to Jane that we would meet after dinner for a game of cards perhaps, in the hotel lounge. But no Jane appeared. I was informed by her sister that Jane had been sent to Coventry which in the case of a person with her disability seemed a strange punishment but apparently, Father had taken a dim view of his daughter allowing her hand to be held and a dimmer view of the youth who had been so bold as to hold it. Mr Jane or Mrs Jane duly informed my parents of the event which had caused such upset and my mother, to her credit, thought it a bit over the top to object, let alone to punish but Jane and her family left soon after and to this day I know not whether the poor young lady ever recovered from the hand-holding incident. I hope she did and that she managed to extricate herself from the over-protectiveness of her father. On the other hand, if any young man dares to hold the hand of one of my granddaughters without my express consent, let alone hers, he will be dispatched further afield than Coventry.

The beach at Muizenberg is where we gathered each day, from morn to late afternoon, doing what the young on beaches the world over tend to do – build sand castles, dig small tunnels, cover their feet with sand, sun bathe and dive into and ride with the waves. Muizenberg tends to be windy so that the heat was often thereby camouflaged, exposing one to the real risk of sunburn. The other risk lay in the water in the form of what we knew as bluebottles which have the appearance of jellyfish and are otherwise known as the Portuguese man o'war. They are small though clearly visible with long thin blue tails and an opaque blue body and are washed ashore in groups, most often when the winds are in a particular direction. Diving into a breaking wave when bluebottles were about could be a truly painful experience.

The Muizenberg Pavilion backed onto the beach, a two-storey elongated construction which housed a cafeteria and a theatre. The highlight of our entertainment at the theatre was Max Collie, the mass hypnotist. Max Collie was a Scot of rotund proportions who sported a moustache and possessed a clear and loud voice. He would invite volunteers from the audience on stage and sit them in a row and snap his fingers, thereby instantly sending them to sleep. He purported to cure smokers of their addiction, and to take individuals back to their childhood so that they spoke as if in their pre-teens. We all had our theories as to how he achieved these feats, wondering sometimes whether he managed to persuade the volunteers to play along, although it is doubtful that he could have succeeded in keeping such a device a secret.

Our suspicions were particularly agitated when our cousin Sam was one such volunteer. Sam, a jolly soul, is one year younger than Henry and they were great mates in Rhodesia. They called each other 'George' which caused some confusion when they were together in the company of the elder members of the family. Sam is in fact a second cousin, the son of Grete, my eldest cousin, the daughter of Simon Stock who arrived in Rhodesia with my parents in the late 1939. Grete was the (first) wife of Leizer Leiserowitz. Grete and Leizer, he much older than she, divorced when Sam was only seven and the father obtained custody, for reasons which were never divulged to me. Leizer spoke with a strong Eastern European accent and gave off an infectious nasal laugh, which Sam inherited. Old man Leiserowitz owned a butchery in Bulawayo along with a Mr Gilbert. The old man remarried, a lady called Beryl who smoked like a chimney, and Grete too remarried, a man called Helmut. Helmut sold lights and light fittings in Salisbury, presumably because it was the more enlightened of the two main cities of Rhodesia. Grete also smoked like a chimney and paid dearly for the habit. But more of Grete later.

Sam wended his way to Max Collie's stage and his performance, when supposedly hypnotised to be a child of about four, was less than convincing, Sam periodically losing concentration and lapsing from baby talk to complex sentence construction, thereby giving rise to the suspicion amongst a number of the audience, most particularly his cousin onlookers, that Sam was faking it and not very adeptly at that. Sam, on one foray into slang worthy of a fourteen-year-old, stumbled onto the credibility issue and in a moment of sheer genius, decided at once to forego the risk inherent in speaking and, quick as a flash, resumed babyhood by sucking his thumb.

After the performance, Sam swore blind that he had all along been 'under', protested that he had no recollection of what had transpired, demanded a blow-by-blow account from us of what childish memories he had divulged to the world at large whilst under Max's mesmerising sway on this, his first stage appearance in Muizenberg and, being sufficiently impressed by the stories we told him, offered himself for a repeat hypnotism the following night. To no one's surprise except Sam's, Max Collie recognised him – the experience had been unusual – and Sam's offer was politely rejected with the excuse that no subject ought to undergo deep hypnosis two nights running.

Then there was a show with knives and swords, in which some troupe from southern Asia frenzied themselves into a trance and stuck swords down their throats and lanced knives through their tongues and came into the audience so that we could at close quarters verify the fact of piercing. One young performer walked the length of the row of seats in which I was seated and in pointing him out to my neighbour, I accidently smacked him in the mouth with my extended pointing arm, which must, for him, have been a painful experience for the mouth which I had struck was wide open and revealed a tongue through which, bleeding a little, was this knife. I offered a fulsome apology which drew no reply which I thought rude until I realised that the encumbrance on his tongue rendered a meaningful response difficult.

Chapter Fifteen

Aunt Emmy was the eldest of the Stock siblings of whom my father was the youngest. On the death of my paternal grandfather, Moses Stock, Emmy assumed the role of matriarch to the Stocks in Lommersum. She married Otto Meyer and they were the first of the Stocks to leave Nazi Germany. They left in 1936 and settled outside Cape Town in an area called Kuils River. There they struggled to make ends meet but meet them they did – Emmy scratched a living baking and selling cakes and biscuits and Otto farmed and made shrewd investments.

Emmy was a short jovial lady with a perpetual smile and a shriek of a laugh, rotund in structure with a large motherly bosom. Otto was genial always, adored his wife, smoked cigars and sported a toothbrush moustache. He was given to venturing definitive opinions on the world of politics, speaking most often in German, excoriating this bloody authoritarian bastard or that, predicting the rise of China long before that inevitably was generally foretold, and advising of the infallibility of investing in gold. In both predictions he proved correct.

In due course they moved from Kuils River to Sea Point, to a bungalow in Gorleston Road, a ten-minute walk to the promenade by the sea front where Otto and Emmy took their daily stroll, arm in arm, past the Sea Point swimming pool with its highest diving board in Africa, off which I once jumped, making the mistake as I did so of leaning forward to see how far I still had to go. I connected with the water whilst my face was still stretched at 90 degrees to the surface, thereby ensuring that my teeth were nearly dislodged.

At Gorleston Road, they had a maid, Ida, who outdid Emmy in girth and had learned from her to concoct the best chicken noodle soup in South Africa. I slurped plate after plate of her noodles and invariably ended my Cape Town holidays a pound or two heavier than when I had arrived.

Emmy and Otto had two children, Max and Lotte. Max studied architecture at Cape Town University and was duly pronounced a qualified architect, which provided his mother with linguistic problems. She was proud of his professional qualification and was bursting at the slightest opportunity to tell anyone who listened that her son was an 'arshitec' which one unkind detractor thought to be a commentary on the artistic worth of the buildings he designed.

Max married Ursula, an attractive dark-haired lady, and he designed for them a house on the slope of the mountain overlooking Camps Bay. To this house we repaired when first it was shown to an admiring family, with its panoramic view of the bay and its swimming pool nestling in the curve of the dwelling area. Robert, their son, was aged about four when my father persuaded him that the main bedroom would lend itself to improvement were he, Robert, to draw on the walls of the main bedroom with Ursula's lipstick. This Robert duly did and Max was faced with a problem of fundamental justice: whether to punish a four-year-old for obeying the destructive and mischievous command of a forty-eight-year-old, or to make a futile demand from the adult for the cost of repainting the walls.

Lotte, a diminutive lady, was the Meyer daughter. She married Edgar Stern from Johannesburg. I have vague recollections of the wedding which took place in Cape Town at the Great Synagogue. We were there and so was the entire Stock clan, from Rhodesia as well as South Africa.

Edgar came from a refined German Jewish family. His parents were refined German Jewish parents with a refined chauffeur who wore a refined blue cap and drove a refined black limousine at a refined pace. Conversations with them were spoken in refined hushed tones and peppered with slight bows and slight inclinations of the head with hands lightly clasped.

I have particular cause to remember the limousine, for I vomited in it. The elder Sterns were kind enough to offer my parents and me, and probably Henry as well, a ride in the limousine around the mountain roads that hug the Cape Town coastline. "Ah," Dad remarked, sotto voce, "what refined people. Frank, remember to look Mr Stern in the eye when you talk to him." This was before I puked. When eventually I puked, looking anyone in the eye was not my main concern. After I puked, looking him in the eye would have required elevation of the head and of dribbled puke on my cheeks.

From Sea Point we drove, in the black limousine, smoothly as the fur on Mrs Stern's mink coat, to Clifton and then on to Camps Bay. I never traveled well in the rear seat and the bends in the road aggravated the nausea. So, increasingly feeling car sick and decreasingly impressed with the luxurious features of the vehicle, I was minded to warn of the impending regurgitation of Ida's most excellent noodles and their accompanying chicken soup, but I felt restrained by the fear that on opening my mouth, my words would be muffled by the act of chundering. I need not have bothered. My mouth opened anyway and it all spewed out in horizontal trajectory, over Frau Lucy Stern's shoulder, down her fur coat, across the back of her leather seat, onto the carpeted floor of the Bentley, with my stomach contents liberally and equitably spread so that ne'er a nook or cranny was missed.

It is a matter of conjecture, though of no practical consequence, whether the greater offence was caused by the mess or by the smell. What was outside the realm of dispute was that the limousine had in that gushing moment lost its refinement, that its occupants were not in royal mood, that the stock of the Stocks in the stern opinion of the Sterns was not as high as it had hitherto been and that the profusion of parental apologies seemed lost on the owners of the car, who had swiftly exited the vehicle and hailed Edgar for replacement transport.

Edgar collected stamps. He specialised in the stamps of the Falkland Islands because, so he protested, he liked penguins and since penguins represented the be all and end all of what the Falklands could offer, their postage stamps were replete with penguins in various poses. To the business minds of the Stock family, stamp collecting was all very well but it wasn't business. Not that stamp collecting was all he did but he wasn't deemed to be a shrewd operator. Little did they know. He went each year to London to a meeting of the Falkland Island stamp collector's fraternity and eventually sold his collection for a fortune, whereupon in the eyes of the family, he instantly became shrewd.

He also had a temper triggered, so it seemed to me, whenever he listened to the news on the radio. He insisted on listening to the news at 1 p.m. and 6 p.m. each day and was determined that when he listened, none should speak, except of course the news reader. On the dot of one or six, as the case might be, he furrowed his brow, blinked his eyelids in rapid succession to add gravity to the occasion, and took in the latest developments in the world with an air of concern and worldly wisdom and woe betide anyone who spoke. "Can I never listen to the news?" he would protest, as if he did anything else. Why he wanted to listen to the news twice each day defeated me and I wondered sometimes whether he only wanted to make sure that there had been no outbreak of polio amongst the penguins of the Falklands; polio, because in the days before the Falk vaccine, polio was a real scare against which we guarded by wearing camphor bags round our necks.

When Edgar wasn't cross, which he often was, he wore a wide smile which seemed fixed to his visage, as if he was compensating for his crossness. So, all in all, he was either shouting or he was smiling; not much in between. Whether he slept with a smile or a frown, I never inquired.

For a reason I shall shortly explain, we saw less of Manfred. Manfred was the only son of Siegfried and Elsa. Siegfried was one of my father's older brothers, a broad-shouldered, straight-backed man with particularly bushy eyebrows. His wife was Elsa, an attractive woman who spoke with a drawl, sported a year-round tan, and went swimming every day at Saunders Rocks, the beach opposite their apartment.

I stayed with them once at that apartment and went swimming in the pool at Saunders Rocks, a pool in the sea, constructed by a low wall against the incoming waves. It was fun to swim there at high tide and to stand on the wall in an attempt to stay upright while the waves rushed over the wall. The water was freezing, since this beach is on the Atlantic side of the Cape, where the water is significantly colder than its Indian Ocean counterpart only a few miles away.

On one occasion, I was standing on the furthest wall, the wall nearest the ocean, that is, with the wind and sun streaming onto my face, the salt-crested waves lashing in, when I was knocked into the pool by a wave but then carried by the retreating wave back over the wall into the sea beyond the pool and onto some rocks. I managed to scramble back into the pool and then onto the beach, exhilarated by the experience until some youth exclaimed that my back was bleeding. Indeed it was. I had apparently cut my lower back against a rock when I was thrown over the wall. I hoot-footed it to the apartment across the road where I was duly tended to by my relatively unconcerned aunt. I still have the scar on my back sixty years on, though the drama of its origin increases with each re-telling.

Manfred was a strikingly good-looking man, also with bushy eyebrows and a penetrating glare, a glare which for most of his waking days was directed at women. He fell in love with and married a French Catholic called Agnes, a blonde beauty. Agnes did not convert to Judaism. A judgment in the

Appellate Division of South Africa, rendered in the course of their subsequent divorce proceedings, records the fact that her parents objected to the marriage because he was a Jew. I suspect it was a toss-up as to which set of parents objected to the marriage most. Family gossip would have it that Manfred must have converted to Catholicism but of this none can be sure. Whatever the case, Manfred had 'married out' and that brought him into ostracism, though whether there was some other cause for the seemingly irredeemable split, I do not know.

But split there was and we never saw Manfred during those years when I went to Cape Town for my holidays. In due course however, the marriage between Manfred and Agnes fell apart and they divorced and Manfred drifted back into the family fold, married again, divorced again and made a fortune in farming and township development, the latter evident from the naming of a street in Belville, Stock Street. He then acquired a farm in Franschoek, the wine region near Cape Town, though he farmed dairy cattle and not wine at a farm from which he could see the prison from which Nelson Mandela was eventually released. And then he acquired a whisky factory which he converted into fine houses. And he became an ardent litigator often, so it seems, just for the thrill of it.

Manfred was renowned for the care he took with his wealth. Not to spend it, that is. It was rumoured that his idea of a suitable present for one of his son's 21st birthday was a bicycle and that in order to test whether any female he dated, after his divorce(s), was more interested in his money than in the man, his form of transport for the lady for a first date was the farm truck. If that put her off, if the reaction was less than passionate, the proof of the pudding was in the eating and there wouldn't be much eating at the designated restaurant.

Yet he relished his return to the family circles and became my favourite cousin, who took practical jokes on the chin and spoke to us with a knowing and mischievous eye which said that he knew that we all shared the same roots. I confess I tested his good nature to the extreme once when, going against his parsimonious grain, he invited my mother, Henry and me and our respective spouses and children to dinner at the Grace Hotel in Cape Town, a hotel of some fame and considerable expense. Frankly, we were surprised by his generous choice of venue and it doesn't reflect well on us that we ordered liberally from the extravagant menu and added stress to our host's sensitivities by persuading the maitre d' to double the bill. Just for a laugh. Given the history of heart disease in the family, it was a risky ruse.

Edgar has long since passed away – or 'passed' as they now say, as if 'away' confers an unacceptable finality upon the event. Lotte lived alone in Johannesburg, and Manfred lived in Franshoek. Max and Ursula moved to Florida and died within one day of each other. And Sam, who went on stage with Max Collie, moved to California where he married Sherry and changed his name from Leiserowitz to Lesser.

Henry's elder son, Justin, moved to London where he thrives as a solicitor and his younger son, Grant moved to Texas where he thrives as an attorney.

My elder son, Daniel, moved to Warwickshire after attending Oxford to study law and my younger son Alexander moved back to Hong Kong, after attending Oxford and Cambridge to study law.

Whence all these lawyers? They are there to encourage litigation, to fulfil Dad's ethos that one of the main functions in life is to sue the bastards.

Chapter Sixteen

Whilst Cape Town was the regular destination for our holidays, there were others. We went once to Durban but the warmth of the Indian Ocean attracts sharks so swimming was hazardous. A teenage Rhodesian girl was attacked there in the late 1950s and although she survived the attack her arm was severed. There were other attacks at about the same time. So that fact and the absence of relatives in Durban made it an obviously less attractive spot than the Cape.

Inyanga, now known as Nyanga, is a mountainous area lying to the east of Zimbabwe. Its topography and climate – cooler – are quite different from the rest of the country, and we would occasionally venture there, staying at a hotel called the Danny Kaye (after the film star) or at Troutbeck Inn. The Troutbeck Inn was, in design and atmosphere, much like that of inns in the Lake District of England; cosy, wooden beams, log fires in winter and studied courtesies.

Lourenco Marques is now called Maputo and is in Mozambique. Dad did business there with a Portuguese cattle man named Bruges. This place was, not surprisingly, Portugal in Africa, charming in its cosmopolitan atmosphere and cuisine and where we first consumed piri piri chicken and stayed at the smart Polana Hotel.

But venturing further afield than southern Africa was seemingly a non-starter not only because of the expense and the attraction of what was at hand but also because Dad had an aversion to any holiday of more than a few days. He was convinced that he had only to leave Bulawayo for a day or two and his whole cattle business would collapse. One week's absence was almost manageable but two or more triggered the spasms in his spastic colon and activated the shaking of the feet syndrome.

The shaking of the feet syndrome was a nervous tick of sorts. He would lie on his holiday bed, wherever that happened to be, and ruminate, gazing at the ceiling, regardless of its architectural merits, chew on a toothpick and mutter to himself with ever increasing agitation. When challenged, he would swear blind that he wasn't thinking of home (by which he meant the farm) and, several times a day, would negate the reliability of that assertion by telephoning – long distance – the farm manager or Gideon the horse supervisor to ascertain whether the cattle were in the paddocks or in the bush; if in the bush, why not in the paddocks; if in the paddocks, why not in the bush; whether the veterinary surgeon had been, if so which veterinary surgeon, how long he had stayed and to what effect, but if not, why not; whether there had been rain, if so whether too much rain, if not when it was forecast to arrive; whether Mr So-and-So had been and if so, what he had been up to when he came, what questions he had asked and how long he had stayed, whether he was returning and if so when; whether the Charolais cow had calved, if not why not and, moreover, why had the staff forgotten to do this that or the other and, invariably, that it took only a day or two for him to be away and the whole kaboodle was a mess and why had he come away in the first place when he had specifically told my mother that it was a bad time to go and then, as predictably as any denouement in a soap opera, the feet, stretching ahead of him and held together, would start to sway rapidly from one side to the other and, damn it, he was going *home.*

So what on earth induced him to take us all to Europe in June 1955, I cannot say.

I was aged ten and Henry fifteen. We flew from Bulawayo to Salisbury (now Harare) in a Dakota aircraft, the kind of small aircraft up the gangway of which one climbed rather than walked and hoped that both propellers continued to propel as far as one's intended destination. At Salisbury we boarded a South African Airways plane, the type known as the constellation. The constellation was recognisable by its three pronged tail.

We stopped first in Khartoum and then in Cairo at about 3 a.m., where Dad decided to have a haircut in the airport building. This turned out to be a bad idea for the method used to deplete hair at that barbershop was the plucking method and a seriously shorn and displeased father emerged, complaining that the man had pulled out his hair instead of cutting it and, even then, one hair at a time, and was this some belated revenge for the ten biblical plagues?

We went to Israel which then was but eight years old and so imbued was I with the novelty of everyone in sight being a Jew that I 'got' religion for a week and wore a yarmulke and ate falafel and went to Mea Shearim, the holy quarter of Jerusalem. No, let me qualify that since all of Jerusalem is almost by definition holy; Mea Shearim is the quarter inhabited by the ultra-orthodox Jew who wears side curls and a black hat and prayer fringes and breeds like a rabbit because it says in the Good Book that one must and anyway by breeding thus prolifically, the time will come, in 2234 perhaps, when the Jew will out-populate any (other) nation so as to lessen the chance of annihilation. And I remember taking a photograph in Mea Shearim when it happened to be the sabbath and hot-footed it out of the alley when a religious nut, no doubt obeying one of the 635 commandments, picked up a stone intending, I surmised, to pelt me to death.

I remember also our sojourn in Italy that year primarily for a plane trip to Milan from Rome. We hit unusually turbulent winds and I spent most of the flight, which because of the storm had to be diverted to Turin, with my face buried in a brown sick bag, making frequent requests to be allowed to disembark in mid-air. I failed to comprehend why this request was denied.

We also went to Germany though why my parents were prepared to put up with the stress and upset which this created, they never explained. We just went where we were taken.

This was a world so different from Africa that I understood, if only briefly, what a wrench the move to Africa must have been for Mom and Dad though I could not fathom why anyone sane would chose to live in such small houses with such small gardens with such lousy weather when the vast expanse of sunny Africa beckoned.

We were a curiosity to the European and, later in the trip, to the Brits as well. We were tanned by comparison, and we came from a distant country about which the European knew little.

What was it like? they asked. Was it very hot and were there many blacks and many wild animals? We made it as wild as credulity could countenance. There was, according to Henry when we spoke to the gullible young in the absence of the adults, a nest of scorpions in our kitchen, a lion cub in our backyard, and a cannibal living next door.

In Deutschland, we visited the village where my father was raised and from which his family had fled. The residents were outwardly friendly but inwardly wary because they didn't know why we were there. Dad maintained a cool distance, venturing only to speak in order to suggest, untruthfully, that he planned to return to set up business again, which scared the hell out of them.

We also visited my mother's Aunt Ella, the only surviving relative she had, though I never worked out by what token she was my mother's aunt. By her or her children I was given two cuddly figures of well-known German characters, toy hedgehogs called Micki and Macki which I dutifully took back with me to Rhodesia, along with a book whose main character was named Struwwelpeter.

I thought Struwwelpeter was a wonderful book with unusual stories of naughty children and colourful illustrations to bring home the horrible things that happen to them when they are wicked. One required a firm disposition to stomach it all. Struwwelpeter himself was a lad who never cut his hair or his fingernails, but there were stories about other personalities too: a boy who ignored his mother's injunction not to suck his thumb and as a result had his thumbs cut off by a tailor with very long scissors; a girl who played with matches and herself caught alight and was reduced to ashes; a boy who tore wings off flies; and the boys who taunted a 'black-a-moor' and were made to realise the folly of their prejudice by being dipped in black ink at the behest of St Nicholas. Good ol' St Nick. Thus brainwashed, the Germans became a nation of manicured and politically correct fly protectors.

In Germany, Mom thought it sweet to buy Henry and me Tyrolean lederhosen. Which we were made to wear. With cute hats which carried little feathers flowing upwards from the sides of the hats, making us look as unbushlike as could be contrived. It wasn't just that we looked embarrassingly ridiculous but the pants were excruciatingly uncomfortable, cutting into the groin. They were made of leather, hence 'lederhosen' and how any male, other than a sexual masochist, could tolerate wearing such stiff pants was beyond me.

I wondered at the time whether this lederhosen and Tyrolean hat exercise was designed to infuse a subliminal disdain for everything Germanic but in fact Mom thought they were smart so perhaps this was her protest at what she perceived to be the lack of refinement in our African lives. There is a family photograph somewhere, in black and white, of Henry and me in lederhosen and felt hats, our hands proudly pushing forward the straps that ran from the trouser waists up our chests and over the shoulders. And we were smiling too. It is as well that the photograph was never put on display in Bulawayo for the probability is that we would have had the shit beaten out of us by the neighbourhood blokes.

I have read somewhere that there is an ailment called ledderhosen disease which is a fungal lumpy infection of the foot. I am only slightly surprised that it has traveled down that far from the crotch.

Then we went to the Black Forest and on to Lucerne in Switzerland and stayed at a hotel, the Burgenstock, overlooking the lake. Here I acquired a taste for mashed banana on toast. As was often the case, I had developed a bout of diarrhea and the remedy prescribed by the Swiss hotel doctor was a diet of whipped up banana, allowed to go brown with age and then digested ever so slowly. I loved it and have since unsuccessfully attempted to interest my grandchildren in this delicacy.

This is where I encountered my first birds and bees lesson, not that I needed one, for, by the age of ten, the boys in Bulawayo were well-versed in these basic facts of life, though not in their practice. Nonetheless, I was by the swimming pool on a lounge chair and next to my mother who was on the neighbouring chair and to her I posed the question of how babies were made.

What the hell induced me to raise the topic, I'm not sure but apparently I smiled as I did so, which drew the query why was I smiling, given that the subject was a serious one and the underlying love between a man and a woman was a beautiful thing. I made some excuse and tried to change the subject but my mother proceeded tactfully to tell me some anatomical facts which she must have found difficult and I so wished I had never asked. The subject was never broached again until I was eighteen and about to go abroad to university, when my mother persuaded my father to 'have a word with Frank.' Dad didn't relish this task and the resulting conversation was short indeed and suffused with vague allusions.

On to London. My first impression of London was of rows and rows of identical houses, unimaginative terraces of dwelling places with close concentrations of chimney stacks. And of pale-faced reserved people whose favourite phrase seemed to be "We must get together while you are in England" with no intention of doing so, not because they were disingenuous but because getting together meant traveling for miles by uncomfortable and crowded public transport.

We went to a suburb called Neasden to meet the Golding family. Louis Golding was an English Jew who had married Emmy Kaufmann and the Kaufmanns were German Jewish refugees to whom we were somehow related. Louis was a mild-mannered gentleman, a law graduate who had gone into local government and in due course become a Conservative councillor. Emmy was a delightful cheerful voluble sort, with laughing eyes and a positive view on life. Living with them were her parents, the Kaufmanns, who spoke only German with a smattering of broken English interspersed, and whose favourite pastime seemed to be watching and commenting upon the weather forecast. They had a particularly keen interest in the weather in Scotland and were in the habit of emerging every now and then from their living room to announce, portentously, in German, that there had been snow in Scotland. The announcement was always brief and to the point and consisted of three words: "Schnee im Schottland!" And as soon as that piece of news was duly assimilated by their astonished audience, they went back to their living room to ascertain from the television what other misfortune had befallen the Scots.

It was there, in London, that we first saw television. Television had not yet arrived in Rhodesia so it was difficult to draw us away from this wondrous contraption, a much smaller screen than is now the common product, with only black and white programmes, ending each night at ten with the playing of the national anthem.

Whilst Henry and I were glued to this novelty, the two Golding children, Anthony and Helen, tried to be hospitable and to glean African stories from us.

Anthony was a year older than I and Helen a year younger. They still are. And there was established by that visit a lifelong friendship and connection with the whole family Golding, a family who showed me infinite kindness and hospitality when I went to England in the 1960s.

Anthony was quite tall and thin; he was intellectual and viewed us with an understandable air of quiet suspicion, as rather odd visitors from a distant shore, which I suppose we were. Since his sister Helen was about my age and intelligent, a well-spoken refined girl and, no mean achievement, Jewish to boot, she garnered constant praise from my father after each visit, he hoping thereby, I have no doubt, to brainwash me into viewing her as a future bride. That I was only ten and she was only nine seemed to him to be irrelevant.

We stayed at the Marble Arch Hotel, near Oxford Street. The highlight of the hotel in those days was The Carvery where, for what seemed a token sum, one could fill one's stomach with large cuts of beef or lamb, mountains of roast potatoes, apple sauce, and several helpings of custardy dessert. There was no occasion for flooding the hotel as there had been in St James or Johannesburg but our bedroom looked out onto a courtyard whereby one could, with a bit of luck, view the habits of those guests in other rooms of the hotel who had not drawn the curtains. Looking out one night, we beheld a young lad in a window opposite engaged in the same fruitless exercise and we exchanged with him a shouted conversation across the void to the annoyance of other guests. He was an American and we invited him to our room for a chinwag only to discover that he had no idea when to call it a night and he stayed on and on despite broad hints that we – Henry and I – wished to retire. I think he was an only child.

We went to Wembley Stadium to watch 'Cinderella on Ice' and oohed and aahed at suitable stages and wondered whether the show might ever come to Bulawayo. I don't think that the idea had occurred to the organisers. Their loss.

The European visit concluded with a trip to Edinburgh to see the famed Edinburgh Tattoo. Though it was summer, it was chilly in Edinburgh but the Tattoo was magnificent and as the lights of Edinburgh Castle dimmed to the sound of the trumpet's Last Post, it seemed a fitting ending to a memorable holiday.

But the adventure wasn't over yet. Not quite. There was the boat journey back. Dad didn't join us on the ship because he had to return home. 'Had to' is relative but enough was enough and the notion of spending ten days on a ship cooped up with families and dinners at the Captain's Table was too much.

What is more, he had been unwell. At about the same time as the novelty of the trip wore off – say, six or seven days into the adventure – he developed a series of complaints which were aggravated, I now dare to suggest, by a dose of recurrent hypochondria.

In June 1955, Dad was forty-seven and pretty healthy, I would say. As good fortune would have it, he lived another forty years. But during the holidays he noticed chest pain and visited a doctor in Israel who foolishly suggested that he might be suffering angina pectoris. The doctor was unaware of the gloom with which diagnoses other than that of the common cold were received. Had he been, he might have acted with more caution before hazarding the angina theory.

The result was a wan expression and predictions of doom, with periodic reminders that the newly discovered disease was the direct result of the stresses of travel and that only a return home to the company of his four-legged friends stood any chance of working a temporary reprieve. Henry, aged all of fifteen, was forewarned, in the style of the Godfather handing over to Al Pacino, that now that he was fifteen, he would be expected, in light of the diagnosis, to assume the role of the head of the family. Henry nodded alarmed acquiescence and wondered what effect this was going to have on finding girlfriends.

So we went on the ship from Southampton to Cape Town, the three of us, Mom, Henry and I. The vessel belonged to the Union Castle Line and there was only one stop, at Madeira. The passengers were of course all white and the staff mostly not. I threw myself into every game in sight and it was on this voyage that I discovered my talent for table tennis. I teamed up with a lad slightly older than I and we entered a knock-out competition. One lady who fancied her chances at winning was so miffed when she and her old witch of a partner were thrashed by these two whipper snappers that she made representations that young persons should not be permitted to partake in competitions designed for adults.

She lost that argument as well as the game and we won a cup, the small mildewed replica of which I possess to this day.

Eventually, alas, we sailed into Cape Town with Table Mountain there to greet us, as was Aunt Emmy with some brown bread and cream cheese in case we had starved on the boat.

We took the train back to Bulawayo and arrived in the middle of a school term, half of which I had missed. So energised was I by my phenomenal trip, that I studied hard to catch up and came second in the term exams. Nehemiah came first. He always did.

Chapter Seventeen

Perhaps it was a rebellious streak in otherwise compliant dispositions that drove both Henry and me to amateur dramatics. I say 'rebellious' because Dad didn't approve. He thought acting to be the preserve of unrefined people. Indeed, so enamoured of the stage was I that, but for this disapproval, my eventual career choice may well have been different.

I started young. My first role was as Joseph in a nativity play when I was at Coghlan School. It wasn't a large role, since Joseph was not the central character, and the passage of time saw him upstaged by his wife, the newborn child, three wise men who intruded uninvited upon the privacy of the rudimentary family abode, and a few goats. But I fared well enough, drawing applause for my attempts to steal the limelight nonetheless. I decided to play Joseph as a cheerful soul, notwithstanding the shock he must have received on discovering that he wasn't the father of the child.

My next stage role was as Tom Sawyer, in a production in which Tom tricks a number of local lads into painting a fence which he has been tasked to paint, even acquiring a dead rat on a string in exchange for the supposed privilege of the paint job. The director provided me with a real dead rat, which I took pleasure in swinging about by its tail, to the evident amusement of the audience and the horror of my parents.

There were no other major productions featuring me at junior school. But there was a radio show which I scripted; not a real radio show but a mock one performed behind some upturned chairs from where a group of us sang a ditty in the form of an advertisement for toothpaste which I called ' 5A Toothpaste' (5A was our class) sung to the tune of 'Davy Crockett, king of the wild frontier'. The toothpaste was said by our song to be so powerful that, like Davy Crockett in his most vigorous escapades, it 'knocked your teeth for a six'. How that allusion was destined to sell toothpaste is a mystery.

I note from the Bulawayo Chronicle (the only newspaper in town) that in November 1955, I was to be seen on the front page in the front row, centre, of a group of schoolboys in Class 3a of Milton Junior School recording a play about Rhodesian history. It was open day at school and the event was seemingly important enough to hit the news. On the blackboard behind us is a chalked map of Rhodesia, with a Union Jack depicted next to Salisbury. What is particularly remarkable about our grouping is that standing next to me on my immediate right is none other than Watkins, Mine-David no less, the argument over his mum's liver seemingly forgotten, and behind us, in between Watkins' face and mine, is Nehemiah Golub. On my left is Robert Ellenbogen and two away from him is a boy holding a stick aloft: perhaps whipping along the horses which drew the wagons of the Pioneers.

The newspaper article says that 'One of the modern ideas employed at the school is the use of a tape recorder for speech training and other purposes.' We were pretty advanced in that regard, obviously. The article also quotes one of the scholars introducing himself as Lobengula, which must have come as a surprise to the boy's parents.

I mention Robert Ellenbogen for two special reasons. The first is that he unwittingly annoyed me whenever we sat exams because I have never encountered before or since any student, at any level, who started writing so swiftly and so furiously as soon as an exam paper was turned face up to be tackled. It was disconcerting, giving the air, as was probably intended, that he knew absolutely everything there was to know about the subject at hand and had barely enough time to scribble it all down. With Ellenbogen sitting next to me or indeed anywhere he could be seen, I found myself invariably panicking to catch up. The second reason is a sad one. He qualified as an accountant in South Africa but succumbed to cancer in his thirties and that left me distressed because he was a gentle soul.

Next in my thespian history was when, in my first year at High School, I was selected, after an audition, to play one of the only two characters in a radio production entitled 'Six Day Safari'. There were six episodes with a story that entailed the older boy and me becoming lost every so often, stranded, and threatened by wild animals in the Okavanga Swamps of Bechuanaland (now Botswana). The studio was a small room at the radio station premises, with microphones hanging from a ceiling, and we were paid precisely one guinea per episode by the Federal Broadcasting Corporation of Rhodesia and Nyasaland. I was something of a hero at school in the weeks that these episodes were broadcast.

In 1961, Milton School staged 'The River Line', a play in three acts by Charles Morgan. The programme cost sixpence and I played the part of Marie Chassaigne, a French woman, who was a member of the Resistance.

Well may you ask why I played the role of a woman. Well, it was an all boys' school, you see, and if the script at hand demanded a female, the part could only be played by a boy. And I was slight for my age, and apparently could pass, if suitably dressed and made up, as a person of the other sex.

In defence of my embarrassment, let me at once disclose that there were two other female roles in the play, each performed by a boy. One was John Hayes who filled the role of Valerie Barton and the other was Gavin McKinley, who played her godmother. John Hayes, you will remember, was the son of Mrs Hayes, our junior school teacher in Class 3a, inhabited at the time of the liver challenge, to which this memoir seems endlessly to return, by Watkins as well. At the back of the programme, there is a 'Thank you' to Rhodesia Railways although the thank you does not state the manner in which Rhodesia Railways contributed to the success of the production.

Once again, the Bulawayo Chronicle zoned in on the act, reporting that a Mrs Suttle was the producer of the play and that she had auditioned many boys for the parts by tape-recording their voices 'and then playing them back before making her choice. This greatly lessens the tedium of selection and is a true medium for testing the quality of voice production.' The invention of the tape recorder was certainly making itself felt in Southern Rhodesia.

One other comment by The Chronicle was to the effect that all three female parts were played by boys and that one of them was 'Frank Stock who did so well as Katherine in Henry V last year.'

Well, alright, I played Katherine in Henry V. I woulds't rather have played Henry or one of the dukes or one of the Welsh soldiers, or even a blade of grass at Agincourt but it was thought that my French pronunciation (for in Act II Scene IV, Kate speaks in French) was sufficiently advanced that I should be cajoled into acting one of the very few female parts in this production, with the sop that in Shakespeare's day, all parts on stage were played by men or boys. The whole of that scene is in French, with ludicrous allusions to the English names of parts of the body and several references to the *grace de Dieu*, of whose *grace* I was sorely in need each evening when venturing onto stage.

The only other appearance which Kate makes in that lengthy production is in Act V, after Henry has soundly defeated the French – we can assume that Shakespeare would not have penned the play had Henry been defeated – and deigns to make his peace by taking her as his bride, whereupon Kate, seeking to impress, tries out her broken English. Henry avows, within about three minutes of meeting her, that she is an angel and that he loves her and cans't she love him too? The answer to which, since he has just decimated her father's army and conquered such parts of France as were not already within England's control, seems something of a foregone conclusion.

I enjoyed Shakespeare, both the study and the acting of it. As in most schools, Shakespeare was central to our study of English literature. The syllabuses for our main exams invariably included a Shakespeare play and in order to bring classroom study alive, it was common practice to stage the current set book piece. I relished the resonance of the language used, the explanations of meanings which were not obvious on first reading, the room created for subtle as well as ringing delivery and the history behind the history plays.

I eventually landed a male role, in fact two, albeit in the same production. It was the musical 'Salad Days' in which I played the roles of Uncle Clam and Professor Zebediah Dawes. This was a far cry from Shakespeare and had nothing to do with any set book.

Although boys were again cast in female roles, there was some novelty in the casting for this particular production which was that two of the headmaster's daughters, Diana and Shane, were in the cast. Diana played the part of Jane and played it very well, with a fine singing voice. Her opposite number in the production, in the role of Timothy, was Giles Ridley, our head boy, a youth of many talents, most particularly cricket and acting. He was a fair-haired, well-spoken lad, upstanding; the archetypal head boy. He went on to study at Cambridge University and then became an actor in South Africa, though not, as far as I am aware, of very wide renown, which surprised me.

Shane played the part of Fiona and I remain amazed that in due course, I dated her. I say 'amazed' because it took guts, I can tell you, to ask the headmaster's daughter for a date and even greater gall to go to the headmaster's house to collect her. I sensed a degree of wariness on the part of her formidable father but it was a wariness which I can now better understand given the advent of granddaughters in my life.

Fetching Shane and returning her home after a night out was effected without the type of embarrassment that befell a member of the Bar in England, according to a much trodden tale, who delivered home the daughter of a judge before whom the advocate was due to appear the next morning. The house was a country house of some size and elegance and the daughter still lived with her parents; in short, it was the judge's residence. The youngish couple had concluded the evening out with a curry at a favourite local Indian restaurant. By the time the two arrived at the judge's house, the curry, probably a vindaloo, had taken its inevitable and inexorable effect. The budding barrister confessed to his date, with all the urgency that he could impart, that he needed use of the washroom. She, appreciating the delicacy of the subject matter, gave him swift instructions as to the location of the required receptacle: a bathroom on the first floor, second door to the right. With barely time to thank her for her understanding, he rushed upstairs, the house in semi-darkness, went to the first floor, thrust open the second door on the right, espied the waiting seat, lowered his pants at speed and did what he had to do with sighs of enormous relief, only to hear the judge's cough from within the water-filled bathtub.

The programme for 'Salad Days' reminds me that in the chorus, hidden amongst the basses, were Brian Kingsley (the youth who had, I think, brought his dog into Ninky Bum's class) and David de Haas (as the confident Constable of France) whose father drove David and me to parties before we secured our driving licences.

I am comforted to see from the same programme that there was a dancing chorus, all boys. I would like to secure the current addresses of the boys who were in that dancing chorus so that I may send to their grandchildren copies of the programme in the hope that those grandchildren inflict the same ribbing as I have suffered at the hands of mine by reason of my female roles at school.

Yet, there was one more. It was the occasion when my talents in Shakespearean delivery were recognised to the extent that I was awarded the best actor of the year prize conferred by the school, a prize that came with no statuette signalling the achievement or even a certificate – merely an announcement in the school hall at an assembly. It was a production of 'Twelfth Night' staged in the open air in the Centenary Park. How we managed to ensure that our voices carried in the open air, I do not recall. But there is, or was, an amphitheatre in the Centenary Park and that is where the play was staged.

I'll come straight to the point. I played the lead role, Viola. Voila!

Mrs Suttle was once again the director. My performance was described in the Year Book's review as forceful and 'beautifully delivered'. In all modesty, I am inclined to agree, remembering with what relish I declared that if only Orsino would reciprocate my affection, I would "[m]ake me a willow cabin at [his] gate; … write loyal cantons of contemned love and sing them loud even in the dead of night. Holla [his] name to the reverberate hills and make the babbling gossip of the air cry out Olivia!" With a breaking down of 'contemned' into three distinct syllables and pronunciation of 'Holla' as 'halloo', I had nailed the meter and commenced to appreciate the genius of Shakespeare.

Sir Toby Belch was a part given to a schoolboy of scant thespian talent yet the part suited him exactly. It was, as far as I am aware, the only part he ever played, on stage that is. His name was Adrian Raucher, a suitably rotund red-faced young man with a notoriously mischievous mien who, in one of the public performances, couldn't resist interrupting the commencement of Malvolio's remonstrances which began "Sir Toby, I must be round with you" by remarking "No need, Malvolio, I'm round enough," a departure from the script which drew immense wrath from Mrs Suttle. When Mrs Suttle was wrathful, it was wise to stand far off.

Other forays by me on stage were shorter, most often on Speech Nights. In July 1959, the guest speaker was the American Consul-General, one Joseph Palmer. The programme was dedicated to democracy and included an extract from the oration by Pericles over the Athenian dead and a rendition of 'Swing Low, Sweet Chariot', though the connection of that spiritual with democracy was lost on me, even then. The choir sang 'Marching through Georgia' and 'Shenandoah', as well, incongruously, as 'The Yeomen of England' and yours truly returned to the American theme by reciting the Walt Whitman poem 'I hear America Singing'.

In 1963, my last year at high school, indeed my last full year in Rhodesia, the theme for Speech Night was the Elizabethan age, which saw me return to Shakespeare with Lorenzo's speech in 'The Merchant of Venice'.

I was in the choir too that night, side by side with Giles Ridley and his brother Chris, another refined member of the Ridley clan and standing not too far from me was my classmate Romy Lis, the 'doofer', whose ill-founded reputation for flatulence neither precluded his membership of a choir nor his subsequent success later in life as a financial guru.

The guest speaker on that occasion was Winston Field, Prime Minister of Southern Rhodesia. He had founded the Dominion Party in the late 1950s, a party to the right of the United Federal Party which had been led by Sir Edgar Whitehead. Fearful of the perceived drift to the left of the political spectrum by Whitehead's party – in other words a drift towards universal franchise – the white electorate voted the Dominion Party into power in late 1961 and in the following year, the party became the Rhodesian Front, with Ian Smith as its deputy leader. The Federation of Rhodesia and Nyasaland thereafter fell apart. In 1964, Field resigned and Smith became prime minister and less than two years later he presided over the Unilateral Declaration of Independence, the pronouncement and consequences of which became world news.

Field conveyed the impression of a serious and respectable politician of some gravitas but was ousted by men of less talent. He died a few years later. But in 1963, he was guest speaker at Milton School. I don't recall what Field said in his speech. Whatever it was, Doofer Lis must have behaved himself, for Field didn't abort his speech midstream. Perhaps by then the choir had moved backstage.

Henry too was given to theatre. His first performance when at Baines Primary School was as the emperor in 'Aladdin and Out', a musical pantomime. This emperor went by the name 'Winky Wum' and was introduced by the chorus singing an unlikely salutation which commenced with the memorable words: 'Oh Winky Wum, we'll beat the drum...'

At high school, he was the headmaster in the farce 'The Happiest Days of Your Life', though school days were not the happiest of Henry's life. He was not attracted to serious study but found his metier in later life in farming with Dad and then in building a successful business of his own in South Africa.

'Arsenic and Old Lace' was perhaps an unlikely production for a school to stage, concentrating as it did on a murderous family, aided by the alcoholic Dr Einstein, played by Henry to hilarious effect, assisted by the fact that he had direct access at home to German accents.

After he left school, he joined the Bulawayo Theatre, an amateur dramatic club which staged, amongst other productions 'The Desert Song' which Henry and his friend Dickie Arbiter helped advertise by riding horseback (on a pair of Dad's horses) through the streets of Bulawayo centre on a Saturday morning decked out in the uniforms of the French Foreign Legion. Dickie somehow found himself in due course as a press adviser to the Prince of Wales (the real one) and has since been seen from time to time commenting on British television on matters royal and wearing loudly awful ties.

The world of theatre will not be remembered for the musical 'Tobacco Time', composed by a Rhodesian with a Rhodesian theme. So forgettable is this musical that those who say that absolutely everything is to be found on Google may be proved incorrect by trying to locate any reference to 'Tobacco Time – the musical'. I remember it only for one number entitled 'Lalapanzi'. Lalapanzi was actually a place in Rhodesia. Indeed, it is still there, called by the same name, which translated means 'lie down'. 'Lie down' describes the village precisely because it is a sleepy one-horse town. However, in the musical there was a university located there, the University of Lalapanzi, which drew a song by the scholars proclaiming the pre-eminence of that mythical seat of learning.

Henry took part in 'Tobacco Time', joined in this effort by our cousin Sam, he of hypnosis fame. Such was the success of 'Tobacco Time' that it was never staged again, so far as I am aware, and Henry and Sam – and Dickie – gave up the theatre for the more serious adventures that adult life presented.

But the Bulawayo Chronicle must have a final say in this segment of my saga. It was theatre of a different kind and one about which my parents were even less enthused than normal. We were living in Fife Street at the time. I was still at junior school and had as yet not made it to the columns of that daily news sheet. That was soon to change.

I had acquired a sound box, a small cylindrical box of the type to be found in teddy bears, with circular holes at one end, whereby a crying or moo-ing sound was made each time one turned the contraption over. And if one turned it over often and quickly, there resulted a rapid coughing sound; if very slowly and quite skillfully, a sound more akin to a moan.

I must have been bored. With this small box, I became an expert in producing a wide range of sound effects of which Alfred Hitchcock would have been proud.

One day, when I was alone at home, I decided to display that expertise over the telephone. I telephoned a number of Bulawayo residents, none known to me – they were random numbers, which was not difficult for in those days there were only four digits per subscriber. When the telephone was answered and a "Good afternoon" ventured, the answerer received a baby's cry, or a cow's moo, or a repetitive cough or a moan or two in response.

I thought that this was quite funny.

One subscriber did not think it funny. He or she telephoned the police and reported the suspicion that someone had been kidnapped and was probably tied up and calling for help.

The police traced the call to my parents' telephone.

The police came to our house. My parents had by then arrived home. They had seen me mess around with the bear contraption and the bear was out of the bag, as it were. The game was up. Never in the history of the British South Africa Police was as abject an apology proffered. This, plus the young age of the offender, plus the assurance of hell, fire and damnation, satisfied the two officers who were perhaps delighted that they did not have to stage some dangerous rescue and off they went.

Hell, fire and damnation duly followed. In addition to whatever sanction was imposed, the verbal tirade was entirely predictable and unending. They (my parents) had not expended all their energies in bringing me up (a strange expression I always thought – as if I were vomit) only to have the police at their door. They (my parents) could not imagine Mrs Golub or Mrs Watkins or Mrs EveryjewishmotherinBulawayo ever ever having to face such a cause of shame from one of their sons and Henrywouldneverdosuchathing (would he not hell).

So I went to bed, hoping against hope that by the morning things would have calmed down.

But I had not counted on the ability of The Bulawayo Chronicle to sniff out everything that went on in the house of everyone in that tidy African town. The next morning at breakfast, the tablecloth was adorned by the usual breakfast accoutrements plus a copy of The Bulawayo Chronicle on the bottom of the front page of which was a headline 'Police alert for kidnapped bear'.

"And not only that," Mom said, as if there had been no pause for breath during the intervening nine hours, "now my son is in the paper. And what for? For getting a prize at school? For something we can be proud of? No, for getting the police to come to our house."

I don't know what happened to my teddy box. But I have occasionally come across similar contraptions since and have played with one or two, fondly as it happens, and I seem to have retained my skill at making all sorts of noises with them, including the noise that someone might make if kidnapped, tied and bound, hand and foot. And gagged.

Chapter Eighteen

Ndebele is the Zulu-based language of the Ndebele tribe who were the indigenous peoples of Matabeleland. Some whites spoke the language itself and very well, but not many. Those who did tended to be farmers and children of farmers who spent their lives in the rural areas. The language was taught as an optional language at some white schools but few availed themselves of that option. It was for the African to learn English if he was to survive economically in the white man's world, not for the white man to learn the language of the majority of the inhabitants. And the extraordinary thing is that it occurred to few whites that there was in this fact something odd, that it was a phenomenon which spoke volumes to the nature of the society they had created.

However, there took place a linguistic compromise of sorts in that most whites spoke a bastardised version of the language.

There were three names given to this language, this form of pidgin Ndebele. It was sometimes called 'Chilapalapa'. I don't myself know whence the title 'chilapalapa' save that 'lapa' meant 'there' or 'on', as in 'faga lapa kitchen' which meant 'put it in the kitchen'. And that brings me to the second name, which is to say, 'kitchen kaffir' – 'kitchen' because – as is illustrated by the example I have just provided – that was the place where it was mostly used to speak to household staff, 'kaffir' because it was used to speak to the African who was pejoratively referred to by those amongst the whites whose thoughts and manners were pejorative, as 'kaffirs'. It dawned on me only many years later that since to Islamists, a 'kaffir' is a non-believer, the etymology of the term which racists used must lie somewhere there.

Thus it was that a white person who espoused liberal, non-racial, views, who favoured, for example, the political advancement of the black, who even dared to socialise with blacks, was scornfully known by whites of a different political bent as a 'kaffir-lover'. Not much different, I imagine, from a term used in similar vein in the American deep south. When in my last year residing in the country, I attended the only non-racial educational institution in the country, a subject to which I turn towards the end of this memoir, I was called a kaffir-lover, for only a kaffir-lover would attend such a place, especially given that he had the choice of attending all white tertiary institutions in neighbouring South Africa.

Alternatively, the patois was sometimes called 'fanigalo', which loosely translated means 'like this'. So, for example, 'enza fanigalo' meant 'do it like this', the standard remark when the employer was demonstrating to the employee how some task or other was to be executed.

Some would say that the use of chilapalapa was disrespectful, because its very nature was childlike. But it was not intended disrespectfully; it was an attempt to bridge a gap, and was quite effective in practice. It was at least more successful than the traditional way in which the Brits seek to overcome language difficulties, which is to speak English to the non-English speaker by articulating each word loudly and very slowly.

It is a fact that I did not myself bother to learn Sindebele and I too used the pidgin form without for a moment thinking it odd or offensive, even though I then considered myself to be sensitive of affronts to the dignity of the African. I expended much of my time learning Latin and French but none learning the local language. And of course there were no lessons in chilapalapa; there hardly could be. There was no grammar to it, no form, no dictionary – one picked it up with the passage of years.

What were its sounds? Most of the words ended in a vowel and the only time I have heard it mistaken for another language was when Henry and I were traveling on the London underground and were using it to converse about two ladies sitting opposite us, when, rudely, we did not want them to know what we were talking about. They looked at us and one nudged the other and whispered, though loudly enough for us to hear, "Italians!" I suppose it sounds a bit like that.

In time, we utilised some of the terminology amongst ourselves, in other words, as between the whites. So, for example, when we were telling someone to hurry up, to get ready for an outing lest we be late, we said "Fagga moto." 'Moto' was supposed to be 'motor', 'faga' was supposed to be 'start', so the combination of the two meant, literally, 'start the motor' but in effect, get a move on, step on the gas. And to convey to the listener that he or a third party was a close friend, it was effective to refer to the friend as 'shamwari'. 'He's my shamwari' meant 'he's my buddy'.

Some of the terms had or have distinctive meanings, difficult to translate or, rather, which carried an effect which is not adequately conveyed in translation. One such was 'hamba gashle' which was a phrase of farewell, telling the other party to go in peace; literally, go slowly.

More often than not, in a conversation which included more than a very few words, English was thrown in when the equivalent in chilapalapa was unknown to the speaker. So if one wished to say: "Put on some boot polish" and didn't know the dialect's word for 'boot polish', the solution was to say "Faga [put] ro ma [the] boot porish." And at other times, the English word was made to sound like a word in the lingua franca itself, as, for example, in 'porish' instead of 'polish', or the expression 'shuwa nyanis' meaning 'really, truly' or 'absolutely certain' where 'shuwa' was a localisation of 'sure'.

Separately, there was Rhodesian slang, occasionally intermingled with chilapalapa.

The Rhodesian accent is significantly less harsh than that of the South African, though there are similarities. The South African accent in the context of spoken English is much influenced by Afrikaans which explains, I believe, its guttural clipped quality.

Rhodesian slang was a manifestation of a relaxed and friendly social environment, far less formal than that of those raised in England, as I was to discover when first I went to the United Kingdom. It was also largely devoid of foul or crude language, another mark of distinction as compared with the readiness with which four letter words were (and are, even more so now) used by the British-based counterpart.

Some expressions do not readily lend themselves to interpretation or explanation, such as 'aag shame', one of my favourites, a knee jerk response, used more by the girls than the lads, when referring to misfortune – even a fairly innocuous one. He has 'flu, or he is struggling with his exams or his dog has died: 'Aag shame.'

An 'O' or 'Ou' (pronounced as in the vowel in 'know') was a male person. Thus 'he's a good ou' meant that he is a good soul, to which the invariable reply came in the form of the question, 'Iz it?' No answer was ever expected when the listening party said 'Iz it ?', for 'Iz it ?' meant 'Is that so ?' and was the standard response to almost any assertion of fact, particularly when one wasn't really interested.

Greater interest in the assertion of fact than a mere 'Iz it?' was to be found in 'Strooze fact?', said with an astonished tone and meaning 'is what you have just articulated really true?' Or one could turn it into support for what one had just asserted, when the accuracy of the assertion was questioned. So, 'No, man, you're kidding' might be met with 'Strooze fact, man.' Which might, depending on the subject matter, lead to 'Aag shame.'

'Strooze God' was a more emphatic version of 'Strooze fact'; it assumed that the greatest truth of all was the existence of God and that conveyed the assertion that the statement in question was equally factual.

'Iz it?' was to be distinguished from 'Howzit?' although the latter was also a question which didn't expect a reply. It was the slang equivalent of 'Hi' or, if you're French, 'Comment ca va?'

'Blerrie' was 'bloody' as in 'blerrie bastard'; 'mooshe' meant nice or well done or pretty (from chilapalapa); 'lekker' meant nice or tasty (from Afrikaans); a 'choom' was a recently arrived Englishman who typically nursed a pink complexion, wore short socks and open sandals instead of calf-length socks and veld schooners and spoke like a … well, like a choom; to 'donner' someone was to beat him (Afrikaans again); 'sterek' meant very or strongly or a great deal (again from chilapalapa); 'for Africa' meant a great number so that 'He has money for Africa' was a statement as to a man's vast wealth.

So a conversation might run thus, to the puzzlement of all English speaking foreigners:

"Howzit?"

"Not good, man. I've just been insulted by John; you know the ou from North End".

"The crazy ou?"

"Yah, he tried to hit me with a hammer ."

"Strooze fact ?"

"Strooze fact."

"What happened man?"

"Well, he said I'd called his chick 'lekker'."

"Iz it?"

"Yah.The he tried to hit me."

"Blerrie bastard."

"So I hit him. Then and there."

"Strooze fact? Iz it?"

"Yah. I donnered him."

"Sterek?"

"Sterek."

"Where'z he now?"

"Bulawayo General."

"Iz it ?"

"All bandaged up."

"Strooze God?"

"Strooze God. He'll need bandages for Africa."

With the softer Rhodesian accent came a softer manner. It was a mark of the average Rhodesian, carried forward to today's young in Zimbabwe, that emphasis was placed on the observance of good manners. It was unthinkable amongst the young not to stand when an adult entered the room. It was commonplace and expected as such to raise one's hat or cap when greeting an adult; and adult men raised their hats to adult men and women on meeting them or on passing an acquaintance in the street. Youngsters called adults 'Sir' or 'Ma'am' and males – adults as well as youngsters – stood up whenever a lady entered the room. Handshakes were firm handshakes, not limp-wristed offerings. And in contrast to the fashion in much of today's Western world, the display of these manners was effected with quiet pride and appreciation. My experience suggests that one of our two school mottos, 'Manners Maketh Man', (the other was 'Quit Ye Like Men') would, in sections of today's West, be met with derision. A pity, since good manners are a sign of civility by which I don't mean modernity; I mean basic civility. In any culture.

A few years ago, I wandered through the grounds of Milton High School of a quiet afternoon. It was the day before the school term started so that there were very few pupils about. Three African students were seated on a bench outside the sixth form block and as I walked past, all three stood, raised their caps and said "Good afternoon, sir." This was not an event I would expect to encounter in school grounds in the United Kingdom, save perhaps at one or two. There it would be considered silly, unnecessary, demeaning perhaps, a relic of a bygone age to be scoffed at as 'posh'. I was gratified by that event, not because I thought myself entitled to be addressed in that manner but, in a world awash with rights and no obligations, their behaviour, in which they took quiet pride, was in itself a disavowal of self-entitlement.

And the emphasis on fine manners stood us in good stead and, besides, was graceful and refined. It stood us in good stead because courtesy breeds courtesy, just as kindness breeds kindness and a smile encourages a reciprocal smile.

I recall with a degree of dismay how it was when I entered a home in England on the day my mother passed away, to use a telephone for an urgent call. The senior person in the house in question was a teacher by profession. And in the house were his children, watching television. The television remained on, despite the news which I brought into that dwelling. None stood up for me. None offered a seat. And so it had been on an earlier occasion when all the seats in the lounge were occupied by youngsters and adults entered the room. Not one youth stood or offered a chair. They lounged there, as was their habit and the habit, no doubt, of their peers. I raised the question of manners with this teacher, suggesting that standing for an adult was a sign of respect, to which his answer was that respect was to be earned; it was not there as of right. Possibly so, but that is a miserable, nihilistic starting point and I know which culture I prefer. And if I have a choice whether to offer a job to a youngster who sees the merit in courtesy and one who does not, I will offer the job to the former, without hesitation. Except there is probably some law now which says that I may not use that measure to make that choice.

I traveled recently on a train in England, from Marylebone Station, London to Leamington Spa. The journey is about an hour and twenty or thirty minutes. When I boarded, shortly before departure time, there were no vacant seats. That was my bad luck but I was content to stand and rest myself against a railing. A short distance from where I stood, was an elderly lady aged, I would say, about seventy-five. She stood and clung on to an overhead bar or rail by a window. Young men were seated, busily engaged on their iPhones. None offered his seat to her and she was relegated to standing and clinging on until, at a stop about three-quarters of an hour into the journey, a seat became vacant. I drew her attention to the vacancy and remarked loudly that in the country which fostered my youth, such a thing would never have happened. I might as well have been talking to sloths. No-one gave a damn.

In advancing these observations, I have been met with the riposte that it would have been better had there been an emphasis, encouraged in the schools, on racial tolerance and decency instead of upon displays of fine manners. Though racial intolerance was never, within my experience, sanctioned at school and I do not think I ever encountered a school master speaking discourteously to a black employee, I do not recall any lessons devoted to the importance of interracial understanding and to that extent the riposte has force. But the value of the cultivation of fine manners is not diminished by a failure to cultivate racial harmony.

That said, manners are sometimes in the eye of the beholder, a fact which was evident in the cultural differences in that part of the world. Thus, habits which we viewed as indicative of good manners might be viewed as poor form by the African, a truth of which the average white, including myself, was generally oblivious.

Late in my sojourn in Rhodesia, when I was already a sixth former, I was invited to a Rotary lunch at which the speaker was, unusually for those days, an African, by which I mean a black African. His theme was African culture and the degree to which the white man's perception of that culture was coloured by a lack of understanding or perhaps a lack of interest in how the other half (more than half actually) lived. The example he gave, which I recall, is that of the Westerner's idea that good manners dictated looking the person to whom one spoke in the eye. That is what young whites were taught. Yet the African viewed that habit, when exhibited by a youth to an elder person, as the height of ill breeding, a show of arrogance, a lack of respect for the elder.

So too, an African's receipt of a gift is not by receiving the object with both hands but by extending one hand – the right – and supporting the forearm of that hand with the left, thereby intimating that the gift has weight, or substance; the right hand is used as the receiving hand, as it is in eating, since the left is for toilet functions.

African food was cooked by our domestic staff on the stove in the family kitchen or in a pot outside over a small fire. It usually took the form of a quite firm white porridge-like substance made of maize meal and they call it *sadza* or *impuphu*. The idea is to mix the meal in a pot with a suitable amount of water and then stir vigorously with a wooden ladle until the water is absorbed and the resulting porridge has achieved the desired consistency. The porridge is scooped in handfuls and rolled or squeezed into a firmness which is then dipped in gravy and taken with meat.

I relished sadza. It was a treat, though I sometimes felt guilty about asking whether there was enough for me to partake. I tended to eat it as an adjunct to a meal which had not sated my hunger. I had the feeling that the domestic staff enjoyed my appreciation of this, their standard diet, but, on reflection, that may merely have been a show of courtesy.

A source of occasional embarrassment, at least to my mind, was the habit of offering staff left-overs from a dinner or lunch which had over-estimated the needs of the employer's family. Again, no offence was intended but I placed myself in the shoes of the donee and concluded that I would be demeaned by the practice.

Even the African handshake was and is different from that of the Westerner. At least so it was in that part of Africa. It was a three-staged process: the first and third stages involved the forward grasping of the hand as in the West but there was an intermediate motion which was to disengage the clasp and take hold of the thumb of the other party's hand. I never knew the significance or origin of this custom which was often preceded, as well as followed, by a single hand clap, as if to signify the glee with which one was being greeted. A search on the internet for some information to enlighten me as to the origin of the habit resulted in an article on the golden handshake given to Robert Mugabe on his supposedly enforced retirement. It was not the handshake I had in mind.

Impuphu was the staple diet of the blacks. The delicacy for the white man was biltong, a dried meat found in elongated flattish slabs, perhaps a quarter of an inch thick and a foot or so in length, either dried in the sun or, more recently, in machines designed for the purpose.

Enter most butcher shops in Rhodesia and there you would see biltong: rows of it hanging on butchers' hooks. It didn't take long to acquire an expertise in alighting on one's slab of choice; not quite as refined an expertise as with wine-tasting but a swifter, more basic process by which one felt the slab for its moisture or dryness, observed it to see whether it was fatty or not, held it to the nose for its smell and asked for a slice of the same batch to taste. It came salted or with spices rubbed in and in beef or game. It was cut into slices or small pieces, either at home or by the butcher on request. We were prohibited from buying the game meat because game is forbidden the Jew by the rules of *kashrut*.

Biltong was not eaten as a main meal or even as part of a main meal. It was to be taken at rugby matches or whilst driving or when sitting on a verandah. It was also eaten at school, when one was not supposed to sneak a piece out of one's pocket and chew away. Biltong could not be swallowed whole; it had vigorously to be chewed which made detection in the classroom almost guaranteed.

Biltong is sometimes referred to as jerky, which is the American term for dried meat in small packets. This is an insult to biltong.

Watching the sun set, chewing biltong and drinking cola tonic and lemonade, was peace and contentment incarnate. Cola tonic is a syrup of reddish-brown hue which must be mixed with lemonade and presented with ice and topped with a slice of lemon. One has to travel to South Africa or Zimbabwe to find it readily available, though it may of late be found in a few outlets in the United Kingdom. It is as refreshing a soft drink as may be found anywhere.

The sundowner represents the quintessential colonial habit in sunny climes of taking a drink after work in a relaxing setting. Where the youngster would take a cola tonic and lemonade or a coke, the adult might take a cocktail. Here was informality at the root of white culture in Rhodesia. The English custom, as I later discovered, was to ask an acquaintance for dinner or for tea three months hence. The Rhodesian habit was to ask the acquaintance to come over for a sundowner that very day and often he would stop by without prior warning. That was the way of things. Snacks might be prepared at a moment's notice and drinks brought out and at some stage of the process, before those present parted for dinner, a silence would descend on the group, just as the sun went down, a silence of friendship and an unspoken appreciation of the continent in which we were blessed to live.

Chapter Nineteen

The day Mr Goldberg held a garden party to mark the completion of his swimming pool was the day Rex decided that he, rather than the host, would be the first in the pool.

Mr Goldberg was a bookmaker and he lived next door to us. When I was fifteen, we moved house from Fife Street to the suburb called Hillside. Hillside is about a mile outside the city centre with large houses and expansive gardens surrounded by bougainvillea hedges. Our move there was a major event. It marked the passage from a very modest home to something quite smart. The house was in Percy Avenue and stood opposite a castle then called Holdengarde Castle, now Nesbitt Castle, a hotel set amongst bush and shrubbery and extensive grounds.

The house to which we moved was a bungalow with a large verandah overlooking an expanse of flower beds and lawn, beyond the hedged border of which was a narrow road which one could cross to reach the Goldberg home.

The Goldberg home was where Max Goldberg resided with his wife Edith and their son Harold, who became a staunch friend. Edith was a member of the Lobel family, a well-known and well-to-do family who owned Lobel Bakery which in turn supplied Lobel bread, perhaps the best known standard loaf in the country.

Mr Goldberg was short and quite round whereas Harold was tall and lanky and a fast sprinter to boot.

Many houses in Bulawayo boasted a swimming pool. Ours did not. So the Goldberg decision to build a swimming pool in their garden met with much anticipation on my part for it went without saying that I would be a frequent user of the pool.

It was a Sunday afternoon. There were tables laid out in the garden, covered with white and flower-embroidered tablecloths and sandwiches and drinks aplenty. The Lobel clan turned out in force as did a generous representation of the friends of the Goldbergs, of whom there were many. Most of us were in our swimming costumes, ready for the plunge, but carefully observing the courtesy of awaiting Mr Goldberg's priority dip.

He was in good form, was Mr Goldberg, smiling at his guests, chatting with them in his friendly and upbeat manner. Harold was also in fine spirits, pacing up and down and biting his fingernails, as was his habit whenever slightly nervous about an event of importance.

Rex was also nervous. Rex was my white Alsatian dog; not albino but white, with a magnificently thick collar of hair and black eyes. He too paced up and down, eyeing the pool with a mixture of suspicion, curiosity and longing. After all, it was a hot day.

The water in the pool was crystal clean, sparkling in the bright sunlight, the surrounding masonry spotlessly awaiting the first bare foot.

No one was allowed to even dip in a toe to test the temperature, for to do so was to deny the owner his preemptive right.

The excitement mounted. One or two of the guests urged Mr Goldberg to dive in or at least to enter gracefully via the steps at the shallow end. Mr G was in a pair of blue trunks and a white towel robe. He cast off his robe. Cameras were at the ready. The moment was at hand.

Rex barked. "Quiet Rex!" I commanded. People laughed at his excitement. He wagged his tail. Then he took the plunge; Rex that is, not Mr Goldberg.

He swam round and round. He was christening the pool.

Mr Goldberg went red in the face. Harold stopped chewing his nails.

"Get that dog out of there!" said Max.

"Who brought that dog here?" asked Edith.

"Rex! Come here boy! Come, come. Good doggie! Good boy!," I shouted to Rex. He ignored me, paddling quite furiously, tongue extended.

Rex was moulting. His white hair came adrift in the crystal clear blue water. It floated over the shallow end as well as over the deep.

One of the Lobel family went to the kitchen and returned with a large bone with some meat attached and ran around the side of the pool trying to coax Rex out with this juicy titbit. But Rex was enjoying the swim. It had been a hot afternoon and as he swam, doggy paddle of course, he took the occasional gulp of the chlorinated water.

Eddie Solomon from next door, a large muscular man, approached with a net attached to a long pole – the type designed to scoop up leaves, not dogs – with which he attempted to garner as much dog hair as he could and when that failed, he tried to poke Rex, and when that failed, he threw hygiene to the wind and jumped in and tried to get hold of the beast. That failed too.

I was by this time receiving dark looks. It seemed entirely possible that if ever Rex emerged from the water and if ever the water became fit for human use, perhaps in a week or two, I wouldn't be allowed to partake of the new facility to which I had been so looking forward. So I jumped in too. The water was balmy and I didn't mind the occasional white hair that ventured towards me. I was tempted to forget about Rex and about Max G and just enjoy the swim but, even submerged, I could hear the shouting.

I swam my best freestyle towards Rex. Rex swam his best doggy paddle away from me. In his excitement, for he thought we were playing a game, he swallowed too much water and coughed out a sufficient amount of saliva as could clearly be seen wending its way to the outlet.

I could hear Harold say to me, as he stood right by the edge of the pool, "Frank, my dad is really cross." This was a rare excursion by Harold into understatement.

Eventually, Rex grew tired and decided that he had had his swim for the day and made his way to the shallow end and gingerly negotiated the steps there, slipping back once or twice.

He made it out, shook himself in close proximity to the ladies who were sipping tea and helped himself to a beef sandwich from a plate which one of the guests had left on the lawn. It was his best day ever.

Harold suggested that we go to his room to watch television. We did. Rex joined us and went to sleep. The swim had been exhausting.

My dogs seemed to have had a penchant for swimming in our neighbours' pools in Hillside. I had another dog, the one before Rex. He too was an Alsatian. He was named Duke. He took a swim one night in the pool of Mr Cassie Weinberg who lived on the side of our plot farthest away from the Goldbergs. Duke nearly drowned because he couldn't find his way out of the pool, which had no shallow end and it was only his yelps which awoke Mr Weinberg at three o'clock one morning that saved his life.

Duke had his uses, though. He is the only dog I know who liked eating untreated horseradish root. One of the rituals observed on the Passover was a distribution of pieces of horseradish root to the diners whilst the elder of the household recounted, as had been the custom for two thousand years, the story of the exodus from Egypt. The horse radish was to remind us of the bitterness suffered by the children of Israel in the course of that memorable journey, though since none of them was asked to eat horseradish during any of their forty years of wandering – a testament to their lack of any sense of direction – I thought the tradition to be harsh on their ethnic descendants. Therefore we took, surreptitiously, to thrusting our morsels of horseradish under the table to the waiting dog and looking nonplussed when, inevitably, he coughed, spluttered and spat them out on the Persian carpet.

Harold was given a car for his sixteenth birthday. It was a Mini Minor, which was made to look even more minor than usual because of Harold's height. His head, when seated, reached the roof so that he had to crouch when he drove.

One was eligible to take one's driving test in Rhodesia at the age of sixteen.

I acquired my driving licence on 28 February 1962, so I was then sixteen years and eight months. I was not the recipient of a car for my sixteenth or even my seventeenth or eighteenth birthdays and I used my mother's green Ford Prefect to take the test.

It wasn't a difficult test, for the roads of Bulawayo were not as jam-packed as those of, say, Bangkok. What was important was to look every few seconds in the mirror and to effect extravagant hand signals, for in those days hand signals were required rather than mechanical indicators to demonstrate to other motorists the intention to turn right or left or to slow down, the last of which was indicated by extending the right arm out of the driver's window and making an up and down motion. Turning right required the driver to stick the arm straight out. Turning left was signalled by an anti-clockwise circular motion with the extended right arm. All this was easy enough save for Sandy Baum, a humorous friend of ours who thought it amusing to conduct all hand signals within the confines of the car cabin itself so that, for example, a turn left was signalled by the left hand outstretched across his passenger's face.

Then there was side parking and then there was reversing between two rows of petrol drums. I caused the green Ford Prefect to strike a petrol drum and was failed.

But no matter, I took the test again the next day, missed the petrol drums and was duly issued with my first driving licence, authorised by the Roads and Road Traffic Act 1953. I paid a fee of one pound and appended my signature to the green booklet which constituted the licence. If I wished, or if

I could not write my signature, there was instead a space for my right thumb print.

The acquisition of a driving licence heralded an entirely new way of life. If one was fortunate enough to persuade one's mother to borrow her car and promise to drive carefully, it was the gateway to dating.

It was also the gateway to the drive-in cinema where dating and driving were all rolled into one.

The drive-in cinema was several miles out of town on the Essexvale Road. The concept was an American import, feasible as an adventure in a country where the evenings were balmy and rain was not plentiful.

The cars were parked in rows, with the front of each on a slight rise and next to a standard pole which housed the loudspeaker set which one hooked on a slightly wound down window of the driver's door. Food was to be had from a central outlet and munched in the car as one watched the movie or watched the girlfriend trying to watch the movie. It was bad form to keep one's headlights on since they lit up the vast screen ahead making viewing difficult.

The end of the show was accompanied by the starting up of many engines and a long queue of vehicles wending their way back along the Essexvale Road into town, there to deliver the girlfriend to the safety of her home with the hope or chance of a kiss to seal a pleasant evening out.

There was also a drive-in restaurant in Bulawayo, the only one, called Fritz's.

Before he opened his drive-in restaurant, Fritz Levy owned a hot dog stall in Grey Street. The hot dog stall was where one went after the movies in town for a hot dog or a steak sandwich and a coke. There was always parking in the street nearby and one ate the goodies either in the car or on bar stools or at one of the two or three tables in front of the stall from which Fritz, with white apron and chef's hat, served his food and drinks.

The drive-in restaurant was more fun for if the diner cared not to dine in the small restaurant area, he parked in the forecourt, flicked his headlights for service and gave the order to a waiter who appeared within seconds by the driver's window and, not too long thereafter, delivered the ordered fare to a tray fixed onto the window.

There were steak sandwiches to be had, steak rolls, and monkey gland steak, a Rhodesian specialty. Now monkey gland steak had nothing to do with monkeys or their glands but was the name of the sauce with which the steak was covered, normally including chutney, tomato puree, mustard, chopped onion and no doubt other sumptuous bits and bobs. It was a wonderful way to finish an evening and the meal was never a substitute for the dinner eaten earlier at home, but always in addition to it.

There were two signs at Fritz's drive-in restaurant: one which had emblazoned upon it the name of the restaurant and the other the instruction on a wall in the forecourt telling motorists to 'Flick Your Lights For Service'. This later instruction did not remain unaltered for long since some wag took it upon himself to use paint and join the 'l' and 'i' in 'Flick' to make the vowel 'U'. No one ever thought to rectify the resulting instruction.

There was one occasion when I did not return my mother's car in the condition in which I entered it on a night out. This was not really my fault.

We went to a party, Harold and I, and neither of us was

used to imbibing alcohol. For reasons which now escape me, Harold gave it a go and by the end of the evening of this party in Kumalo, he was the worse for wear. It fell to me to drive him home, not surprisingly since we lived next door to each other and I had my mother's Ford Prefect with me.

So we drove home from Kumalo to Hillside, not a long distance but on that evening it was a long drive; for every ten yards or so, Harold ordered me to stop the vehicle so that he might disembark and see if he was about to regurgitate the evening's meal. Sometimes he did, sometimes he didn't. But we soon became tired of stopping the car so often. So we stumbled upon the idea that whilst I drove, very slowly, Harold would keep the passenger door open and if needs must, aim the contents of his stomach in a respectable trajectory onto the road as we went along, past the General Hospital, past the lunatic asylum, as we knew it, and down the Essexvale Road to Percy Avenue. Sometimes the trajectory succeeded in missing the door frame of the car, sometimes it didn't.

Henry acquired a car after he completed his schooling. It was a black Ford Falcon, registration number RB 10. 'R' stood for Rhodesia and 'B' for Bulawayo. How he managed to secure the distinctive number 10 I cannot say but it added somehow to the lure of the vehicle of which he was sufficiently proud to forbid my use of it.

One distinctive feature of country roads in Rhodesia were strip roads. Negotiating strips required special skill not least if one was traveling at speed. The strip road consisted of two parallel strips of tarmacadam with dust in between and on either side. The strips are so distanced one from the other as to enable the nearside wheels to occupy one strip and the offside wheels to occupy the other. So in effect, as far as the wheels themselves were concerned, they were using tarmacked road. But it was not as simple as that because the roads catered for, and expected, two way traffic. And if two cars were traveling towards each other – more often than not at high speed, given the paucity of traffic in the bush areas – neither vehicle could expect to enjoy use of both strips for too long, for to do so was to invite a head on collision. One or other of the vehicles had to give way. The answer lay in a hair-raising compromise whereby each vehicle moved over to the left so that the offside wheels moved along one strip and the nearside wheels negotiated the nearside dust, thereby ensuring that each vehicle passed the other at perilously close quarters and thereafter returned to occupy both strips.

This was fun and by its nature tempted the young driver and the not-so-young to engage in hair-raising games of chicken. Accidents were remarkably few.

The journeys taken by the teenage driver harboured a number of imperative destinations apart from the drive-in cinema and the drive-in restaurants. One regular haunt was the Dairy Den, an ice cream parlour on the Hillside Road. The Dairy Den, close to the music school, and the trade fair grounds, was a place of social gathering and the ice creams were secondary, though certainly delicious with large vanilla ice cream cones and flake chocolates shoved inside.

Next were the Hillside Dams, a half a mile or so from our house in Percy Avenue, a wonderful retreat for family Sunday strolls and picnics.

But the nights at the Hillside Dam were not family nights. It was the destination for young couples who desired a degree of privacy after a night out, though the police were seasoned spoilers in this regard and privacy was often interrupted by the headlights of a police van which obviated the need for a policeman to approach the romantic couple and ask them to move on. It was difficult to understand who it was who might be offended by these trysts. No one ever complained about these police intrusions, there were no letters to the papers about it and no challenge based on constitutional rights to privacy. It was just assumed that the police were entitled to do what they did and I suppose the embarrassment of being asked to move on in such circumstances sufficed to kill the temptation to go there again. At night, at least.

Chapter Twenty

No account of one's youth would be a complete account without reference to girlfriends. It is not an easy subject to approach at the evening of one's life given the knowledge that what I write may be read critically by several closely interested groups. One's wife, for sure, one's offspring and, possibly, but not least, the girlfriends in question. It is on any view a delicate subject and I think it prudent to change names lest some former girlfriend now finds herself married to a serial killer.

I landed my first girlfriend by an exercise which would make me the darling of the modern women's rights movement, for my reticence and the democratic manner in which the exercise was broached and concluded.

Let us call her Miranda. She was (is) Jewish which, for a start, was unusual for me. She had dark hair, was slightly built, and a cheerful lass. She was taller than her parents which was no signal achievement given that her parents were diminutive. Be that as it may, the time came when she was given a choice. Andy or me. No wooing. No flowers. No promises of love, undying or otherwise. No commitment to take her to the ice-cream parlour or the movies. Just a democratic choice. Hers. And we would respect her wish without a second's hesitation.

Andy was one of my best friends. He liked Miranda a lot and I suppose so did I. We both wanted to hold her hand, albeit not at the same time, and maybe steal a kiss. I don't recall how old we were, but it was early in our passage from boyhood to teenhood.

Andy was shorter than I and skinnier, which is saying a lot because I was truly skinny. He also had webbed toes though I doubt that this influenced Miranda. Exemplifying the cruelty of youth, we called him 'Froggy'. He had a wicked sense of humour and was effervescent, so to establish a contrast I affected an air of quiet maturity.

It was an unspoken understanding that however our objective – Miranda – was to be wooed and won over, a punch-up was off the table. There was only one way to resolve an issue which was causing both of us to lose sleep, though not too much because in truth we were not overly fussed about the possibility of losing.

We decided to cut the gordian knot by telling her, in each other's presence, that we each wished her to be our girlfriend and that she was requested to choose between us. She was to make her choice there and then without hearing contending submissions and without providing reasons for her choice, lest those reasons proved painful to the loser. It did not occur to us that she might not be interested in either of us, that she might laugh at the idea, that she might say that she was flattered but no thank you very much. She just had to be interested in one of us. Who else in the world was there ?

It was a lazy Saturday afternoon at her parents' house. Andy and I were suitably attired in our shorts and besmirched with dust from a game of marbles in the back yard and she was looking upon us benignly from the verandah that encircled the bungalow.

We spoke to her directly. We explained the rules, at the very same time advancing the marbles contest, and she looked from him to me and back again and perhaps because he was covered in more dust than I and, she being quite a tidy and germ-free sort, she selected me.

That settled, we continued our game of marbles.

I can't remember whether in fact I ever got to holding either of her hands or to kiss her, which is not to derogate from her attraction. It's just too long ago and obviously she didn't take centre stage in my young life. She married someone else in due course, which came as no surprise since it was about ten years later and our rather tenuous bonding had lasted roughly two months, perhaps less and, anyway, Andy emigrated for reasons quite unconnected with Miranda's choice, so the feeling of success at the expense of another thereupon dissipated.

When still too young to secure driving licences but old enough to be allowed to go to a party on a Saturday night, arrangements were always in place for a parent to drive us there and fetch us, which made dating impossible. The embarrassment that came with a father in the driving seat whilst the son was trying to impress the girl was too much. It just didn't work.

But occasionally, this arrangement provided a recipe for disaster.

David and I were good friends. We still are today. Not the David of Watkins fame, but another David; although I hasten to say, in case he still wants to thump me, that I have nothing against Watkins. Anyway, the David of whom I speak was also born of German Jewish stock and his parents and my parents, though not close friends, regarded each other with respect. His father was an upright personality; a little stern perhaps, or so it seemed to me, but always cheerful enough when he saw me.

David and I went to a party. I can't recall whose party but it wasn't a party of the Kumalo crowd. David and I didn't belong to the Kumalo crowd. The Jewish boys of Kumalo were, by and large, a different breed; somewhat more advanced in their exposure to members of the opposite sex, financially well off and a rather spoilt but confident group with whom we didn't really fit. I think they thought us weedy. Which in a sense we were, if you assessed strength in muscular terms but I believe we had our own charm and oodles of fine manners into which we were inculcated by our Western European heritage. The fine manners stood us in excellent stead with the parents of the girls and, through the positive comments of the parents, with the girls themselves.

The girls across whom we stumbled that particular evening were, let us say, of Turkish origin. They were not in fact Turkish but of another origin but I am loathe to get even close to identifying them, lest their father is still alive. Or maybe they have brothers. or big cousins. And, to emphasise anonymity, I'll say Turkish because I am not sure there were any Turks at all in Bulawayo. And although there were, as in all the sects which inhabited our community, many in Bulawayo of refined reputation, this particular family was, we later discovered, not amongst that breed. They were a bit rough.

Quite what motivated David and I to make a beeline for these particular sisters, only heaven and David and I know. Perhaps it was the overweening power of their perfume or the fact that they were not overly fussy about their choice of dance partner that proved the attraction. Anyway, we danced with them and they danced with us.

These were the early years of rock and roll. The twist. The Madison. The camel walk. The slow dance when the beat, if there was one, was irrelevant. Maybe we danced to the tune of 'The Lion Sleeps Tonight' with its recurrent 'a-weema-weh a-weema-we', whatever that meant. Maybe we feigned interest in Turkish culture. Maybe we had lost touch with what was sensible, for one of us – I like to think it wasn't me – offered them a lift home.

This was a strange thing to do, given that neither of us possessed a car. Maybe we thought we could kiss and cuddle in the back seat but given that David's father would be the driver, and that the back seat didn't accommodate four, that could hardly have been the reason.

There were several facts of which we were not aware. The first was that it was late; say 11.30 p.m. The second was that the girls had been given a curfew. 10 p.m. The third was that the father of the girls was given to drink. The fourth was that this night was no exception; he had been drinking since, I would estimate, 5 p.m.

One fact of which we were aware, however, was that David's father was a particularly well-mannered man. This dictated that when we arrived at the house in which the girls and their father resided, David's father insisted on seeing the sisters to the front door.

That was not a good idea.

The father of the girls, fired up by drink, put together in his inebriated mind the lateness of the hour and the age of the man who had been with his precious offspring of tender years in a private vehicle and concluded, in a singular miscarriage of justice, that this embodiment of Germanic culture was in fact a pervert.

David and I all the while, with a sixth sense that not all was going to turn out well, stayed pinned to our car seats which were hidden in the darkness of the night.

The event was short but the message was clear. In answer to the polite "Good evening" which David's father ventured to Mr Turk, who was barefoot and adorned only in shorts and a crumpled vest which had seen better days, Mr Turk punched David's father in the nose.

David's father was not the pugilistic type. In any event, his nose was sore. And, further than that, the punch having been delivered, the door was slammed shut. So there was no retaliation offered. Not toward Mr Turk at least. The retaliation was reserved for David and me.

By midnight, I had been delivered home. I was then living in Hillside, in Percy Avenue, quite near David's house. I thought it wise to go straight to bed. My parents were asleep. Not for long. David's father, now nursing a nose whose size was increasing by the swelling minute, was sufficiently put out to telephone my father and discuss what had happened and what should be done.

Needless to say, I was in for the high jump. I thought this

a little unfair, given that it had not been I who had struck the old man's nose. But apparently this was not the point. The point was the type of lass with whom I had chosen to consort. Not only was she not Jewish, she was from a family of low repute, an unfortunate combination.

The matter was never reported to the police nor were civil proceedings, claiming damages for assault, instituted. To do either would merely draw attention to our disgraceful behaviour.

As a postscript, David insists to this day that there were not two sisters, that there was only one daughter, that I had alighted on her, that I alone was responsible for the lift home and the resulting punch and that he was but an innocent onlooker to a disaster of my own creation. He may be correct. But the kernel of the story is true.

Then there was Jeannie, my first affair of the heart. I first saw her when I was enrolled in the school musical 'Salad Days'. She was from Eveline School, an all-girls school, something of a sister school to Milton. She was doing make up for the play, and when my eyes first alighted upon her, she was frizzing up the hair of the headmaster's beautiful daughter, Diana, who took the female lead.

Jeannie's was an easy temperament, with a cheerful smile and a pleasant face and she was my girlfriend for the last two years I was at school.

By the time we struck up a relationship, I had passed my driving test so our dates were made easier by my mother's willingness to lend me her Ford Prefect with which I would fetch Jeannie from her parents' apartment in town, to go to the cinema or to go to parties or to go on treasure hunts on a Sunday.

Her parents were Liverpudlians and they lived in modest accommodation. I think that her father worked for Rhodesia Railways, though in what capacity, I cannot say. Oddly enough, although Jeannie was not Jewish, my parents did not object to our dating. My mother, in particular, liked her.

Jeannie eventually went to Natal University and I think she married a farmer in Rhodesia but I don't know what became of her. Her name never appears in any list of names in Rhodesian websites. I hope nothing bad happened to them in the days of guerilla warfare.

Parties were relatively respectable affairs. There was little drinking of alcohol and drugs were never in the picture. Dancing was of the cheek to cheek variety to hits such as 'Moon River', 'Stand by Me', 'Unchained Melody', 'Are You Lonesome Tonight', 'Stranger on the Shore', 'The Great Pretender', 'I Can't Stop Loving You', and 'Crying in the Rain', and of the Be-pop variety to faster numbers such as 'Runaway', 'Let's Twist Tonight' and 'The Loco-Motion'. 'The Lion Sleeps Tonight' was always a favourite, evoking the Africa in our bones. It still takes me back to those halcyon days. 'Wooden Heart', sung by Elvis Presley, was a popular tune which had special meaning for me because Mom knew the tune when first it came on. It was an English version of an old German folk song 'Muss I Denn' in which the singer bemoans the fact that he has to leave his damsel behind – must he really leave the town and must it be that 'du mein Schatz bleibst hier' ('you my sweetheart stays here?'). As much as I baulk at the sound of the German tongue, I preferred and sang the German version. Elvis' wooden heart didn't carry the same message or ask the same eternal question. And my mother's heart was, for a moment or two, wistfully carried back to happier days.

It was a fact of life that parties which we attended were all white affairs. We simply didn't socialise with black youngsters for, despite the strength of feeling amongst some of us that racial discrimination was abhorrent, our circles never crossed paths socially. Schools were not mixed and our social circles centred around our school friends. Times would in due course change but not in the 1950s or sixties.

Dates were often excursions to the cinema to which the advent of technicolor was an exciting development but not nearly as exciting as Cinerama. Cinerama described the screen, an elongated and curved widescreen and it was an event, an excitement in itself which for a month or two took one's mind off the imperative of holding the girl's hand or even securing one's arm around her shoulders.

An outing at the cinema or to a party was almost invariably followed by a late night meal at the Oasis restaurant in town. Not a smart restaurant – funds didn't run to smart – but good food of which my favourite was their Vienna schnitzel. It had the feel of an American diner and was far from romantic. Romantic was an Italian restaurant called Nick's where one hand was stretched over the red and white check tablecloth trying to locate the girlfriend's hand in the near dark, the other nervously fondling the wax dripping from the candle between the couple.

Or there was always Fritz's drive-in restaurant,; the place where one flicked one's lights for service.

And there was also the Dairy Den, not a night time haunt but a place for the young to gather and enjoy the best ice creams in town. Perhaps the only ice creams in town.

I saw 'Gone with the Wind' with the headmaster's daughter but that was not a lengthy romance, delightful young lady though she was. Jeannie remained the centre of my affections.

Because the town wasn't large and the white population was small, an outing with a girlfriend was soon common knowledge and at times gossip, especially when it came to the dating record of the Stock brothers.

It was an unspoken rule that Jewish boys dated Jewish girls. But, to the chagrin of our parents, Henry and I saw it differently. I don't think that this was a rebellious streak in either of us. Perhaps it was more a product of the fact that the Jewish girls moved with the Kumalo crowd of which we were simply not part. And of course by widening the net, we widened the choice.

In due course this brotherly habit led to major and serious problems on the parental front, for what was feared was that one day we might consider marrying outside the faith. That notion was more than simply taboo, especially for parents who, from their dreadful experiences of anti-Semitism, took the view that when push came to shove, when first a crack appeared in the ranks of matrimonial harmony, the non-Jewish wife would call her husband a bloody Jew. That has not been my personal experience, far from it, but that was the expressed fear. To which was added the 'what would people say' consideration and the conviction that a Jewish family life was a life of warmth and ancient cultural traits which were alien to the non-Jew; or perhaps, put another way, that to marry within the faith was to marry a commonality of experience which could only work to the benefit of an institution which carried sufficient perils without importing clashing backgrounds.

The Chinese feel the same. They too, for much the same reason, much prefer their sons and daughters to marry other Chinese. And I imagine the Greeks and other tribes too.

Come to think of it, I vouch that some non-Jews prefer their sons and daughters not to marry Jews. Years later when staying at a bed and breakfast place in Wiltshire, our hostess, an elderly English country lady, spent the evening showing us her family photo album. One photograph was of her daughter who lived in India. "Her husband is a Jew, you know," she revealed and added, with a sigh, "But he's quite nice really."

Chapter Twenty-One

Living in Hillside, from the age of fifteen, was idyllic. Our house there, in Percy Avenue, was an L-shaped three-bedroomed bungalow with a large garden overlooked by a stoep or verandah where we would sit on balmy evenings of which there were many in a country which has one of the most pleasant climates on Earth.

Waking in the mornings was waking to bird song and crisp clear air and riding one's bicycle to school at about 7.30 a.m. which was a fifteen or twenty minute affair on dusty cycle paths, a feat which I mention in the same breath as the weather since the ride was a refreshing way to start a day.

The rainy season was from November to March but the rains were spasmodic rather than continuous, comprising, in the main, heavy afternoon thunderstorms of an hour or so, after which the smell of the earth changed and the skies cleared with the possibility of a storm at night as well.

Winters were cool, not cold, and it never snowed. In the winter, our school uniforms changed to grey from khaki and to caps rather than hats.

Harold lived next door, across the pathway between the two houses and we ventured to each other's abodes as the mood dictated, although table tennis was always played on the verandah of 'my' house.

Our table tennis championships were grand and prolonged affairs because we staged imaginary world knockout competitions whereby we would draw tables of 32 or 64 countries, decide on seeding (using as a yardstick the assumption that world powers were likely to be more talented than the obscure) and which of us would represent which countries.

And so the competition commenced in deadly earnest, mostly of an evening, spread over several days.

And each match was accompanied by supposed radio commentary provided by whichever one of us was winning at a given moment. We were closely matched, so the excitement was considerable and commentary was suspended, to avoid embarrassment, only when an adult or Henry came into view.

Harold was a slim, tall, lanky sprinter. He excelled at school sprints but his possible career in that department was curtailed by a mild heart-related condition.

I was slim but neither tall nor lanky and I certainly couldn't sprint but in table tennis I discovered the only sport at which I could realistically compete.

I played tennis though. At school. Not in a school team but I went for tennis coaching nonetheless on courts located behind the Sixth Form block. I had a wooden racquet. We all had wooden racquets purchased from the only sports outlet in town, Townsend and Fletcher.

Swimming pools, both public and private, were all open to the elements. There was no such thing as an indoor pool since the weather was too fine to justify one. Our favourite public bathing pool was the Borrow Street Baths, set back from the main road, and to this enormous pool surrounded by lawn and tall trees we wended our way as primary school children for Milton Junior School possessed no pool of its own; it was only the High School that had constructed a pool but it didn't have the charm of the Borrow Street Baths.

It was unheard of for a youngster in Rhodesia not to learn to swim and I, like most others, took private swimming lessons though I was no great swimmer and the temptation to show off a muscle-bound thorax was not open to me since mine was not muscle-bound.

I do not know what caveman instinct dictated that whenever in a boys' changing room, the bigger chaps wet the corner of their towels with which to flick the hides of the smaller chaps. It was a routine, a rite of passage, to which we subjected ourselves every week, without objection or protest, though I wondered what career path for the flicker and for the flicked, respectively, this pastime betokened. Perhaps some of the flickers eventually ran training schools for water-boarding suspected terrorists and the flicked became plastic surgeons in sympathy with hides that merited repair.

So much for sport at school, save that the choice of prefects was restricted, or so it seemed, to those who excelled at sport. The head boy was either captain of the first XV cricket team or a member of the school's rugby team, or both.

This meant that the chance of my appointment as a prefect, which amongst other advantages conferred the right to wear a light grey blazer and a prefect's tie and provided a passport to caning other school boys, was non-existent.

I was however elevated to the lesser station of library prefect. This is not an honour of which I have bragged in the course of my life and does not, as yet, appear in any of the many curriculum vitae which over the years I have drafted. Being a library prefect – an appointment which took effect when I reached the sixth form – entitled me to sit behind the library counter, stamp whatever had to be stamped when a sixth former borrowed a book, and maintain discipline. Maintaining discipline was the entitlement rather than the practice. It was supposed to consist of making sure that there was no talking in the library and I was even accorded the power to expel chatterers from the library. I have, vicariously, made up for this miserable lack of prefecture attainment by marrying a lady who was head girl of a well-known grammar school.

Television was introduced to Rhodesia only in 1960 but imported into our household later than that since it was thought, with some justification, that television was likely to distract from school work. So I was relegated to catching the odd programme over at Harold's house.

Favourites were 'The Beverly Hillbillies', 'Bootsie and Snudge', 'Have Gun – Will Travel', 'Bonanza', 'The Addams Family', and 'Rawhide'. 'Gunsmoke' had as its main character Matt Dillon, a US Marshal with his sidekick Chester, who walked with a limp which always reminded me of Mr Adams' leg and there was a tendency amongst the school boys on the morning after an episode to walk from class to class with an exaggerated limp.

Leisure time at home was, in the absence of television, devoted to reading or listening to the radio or to music on vinyl discs or, occasionally, to Mom on the piano.

My taste in books was relatively eclectic but those which stand out are 'The Thirty Nine Steps', '1984', 'On the Beach', 'The War of the Worlds', 'The Wreck of the Mary Deare' and anything by Alan Paton. 'On the Beach' was written by Nevil Shute who was also the author of 'A Town Like Alice' in which 'Alice' is Alice Springs in Australia. I had the dubious privilege years later of entertaining two New Yorkers whose worldview was not a world view at all but, to the contrary, somewhat parochial. When I told them that I had recently returned from a visit to Australia, they proffered the extraordinary suggestion that I must have found Australia primitive. My assurances that I had instead encountered a culture which was, by any standard, sophisticated were brushed aside on the basis that they knew better for they had seen a film based on a book and set in the outback of Australia, the title of which they (mis) remembered as 'A Town Like Nancy'.

'Jock of the Bushveld' was a southern African classic, first published in 1907, a tale of a bull terrier, a hunting dog, told by his master. Together they experience adventures in the bush, a yarn tailored for those enamoured of the African wilderness though some its allusions would now, a century later, be accepted as offensive as in the tale about Jim Makokel', a strong Zulu, who had fought with his tribe at Rorke's Drift against the white man and comes to find himself in the employ of the narrator and befriends Jock; Makolel' holds himself, as a Zulu, a cut above the rest of the indigenous African who are viewed by him disparagingly.

Mom and Dad loved opera and it was in that context that we came to know and appreciate the great operatic voices of the era, most particularly Benjamino Gigli and, Dad's favourite, Jussi Bjoerling whose voice I still regard as the sweetest of all. Mario Lanza was much in vogue but hardly up to Bjoerling's standard. We also listened to the records of Richard Tauber and music from the shows such as 'Gigi' and 'Annie Get Your Gun', and, when left in the absence of my parents, to the yodelling of Frank Ifield and the Platters singing 'The Great Pretender', the last of which encouraged my imagination to foresee the day when I would be singing the self-same number to vast adoring crowds. Shut in my room, curtains closed, a corn on the cob as a microphone in hand, the Platters as a backing group, my copper-coloured table lamp as a singular spot-light, I was the Great Pretender, even ending my performance by mimicking the approving roars of the audience, all adulation, only to be ruined by being told by Mom that dinner was ready.

Opposite my bedroom in Hillside was a toilet; not a bathroom with a toilet but a cubicle of a room housing only a toilet. The seclusion and quiet offered by this tiny room was ideal for studying, or at least so I found. Since using the toilet seat whilst studying was not comfortable, I stumbled upon the excellent notion of importing a small fishing chair, the seat of which was no more than nine inches or so from the ground, and resting my papers on the floor and on the closed toilet seat itself. Air was a bit restricted and the tiny high window let in a minimum of natural light but the bulb made the necessary difference and here I would ensconce myself, sometimes as early as 4 a.m. whilst the house was asleep and study in anticipation of my 'A' level exams. I have never since discovered a more conducive place in which to concentrate. It had the added advantage that time off to go to the loo when nature called was kept to a bare minimum.

School examinations were much like school examinations elsewhere I suppose. The major exams – the Cambridge School Certificate and 'A' Levels – were held in the school hall and I am proud to say that I had spent so much time in the loo whilst preparing that I never had occasion to seek leave for a toilet break during exams; I was, by then, dried out.

I remember two things in particular about my school exams: one was my habit of underlining passages in red whenever I was stuck for an answer so that none casting his eyes about would see me idle and realise that I was stuck, and the other was the day, during our Cambridge School Certificate exams, when the father of one of my classmates took it upon himself to commit suicide. He owned a furniture store in town. Whether that had anything to do with the decision to shoot himself, no one knew, but the timing was certainly tough for his son who pressed ahead nonetheless with his exam although it was said that a note was written to the examination board drawing to its attention the disadvantage under which the candidate's labours were exerted. We were sufficiently imbued with the British sense of fair play not to begrudge him that consideration. Even sadder to relate is the fact that much later in life, the son took the same course by casting himself under a London Underground train.

I did well enough in my School Certificate exams, surprisingly so in maths and the sciences which had never been as appealing to me as the humanities. I did not, however, fare well in my 'A' levels even though well enough to gain entry to university. The disappointing results were largely attributable to the choice of subjects I was erroneously persuaded to take on the misinformed basis that they were useful subjects if I was to study law. They included Economics and Economic History. The only connection between those subjects and my leanings was the word 'economic' for that described exactly the extent of my interest in them. I would far rather have taken French and Latin, though I did take Latin for what was called 'AS Level' and enjoyed it, despite the fact that the examination in Latin was disconcerting since the set book paper was based on a book which had not been set for us, an omission the cause of which remained a mystery. This mishap resulted in another letter to the examining board asking that our attempts be treated as translations of unseen passages. It worked and we passed, though not with brilliant colours.

Our economic history course included a study of early capitalism in the cloth trade, for heaven's sake; agricultural regulations in Tudor England, would you believe; the West of England cloth trade, in case the connection between cloth and wealth had not sunk in; the defects of competition, when all around me was competition to do better than the next man; a study of the distinction between woollen trades and worsted trades, an issue which didn't keep me awake at night; the difficulties of constructing canals, which was likely to be of scant use in life at the Bar unless one developed a specialist canal practice; and the sanitary conditions in Bolton and Bradford, in case one forgot what a shit subject this was.

This was a far cry from life at the Bar as I envisaged, and later experienced, it. I had, long before the dreary periods listening to Sandbags teaching me economic history, determined to go to the Bar. Advocacy for me had the allure of theatrical battles for justice.

I had watched Perry Mason winning all his cases, even from the disadvantageous position of his wheelchair. I had read Louis Nizer's 'My Life in Court' (don't ask who Louis Nizer is, I never came across his name again); and I had cross-examined my distant cousin Wolfgang in the lounge of our Fife Street home for hours on end, having first made sure that the script was tailored to ensure flights of oratory by myself, monosyllabic answers from the witness and a silent jury driven by my brilliance to acquit my innocent client (he was invariably an innocent client). Since Wolfgang, recently arrived from Germany, was learning English and since he was a guest in our house, linguistic handicaps and basic courtesy rendered hopeless any thought of protest on his part.

In my later school years, I started frequenting the High Court in Bulawayo to observe trials. The High Court building was an impressive domed colonial structure somewhat majestically overlooking the length of 8th Avenue. It housed two courts, one on either side of a quadrangle. The interiors of the courts were quite dark with much wood panelling and the only thing that was guaranteed to be white were the judges and advocates.

The litigants, in the main, were black, and many were from the rural areas so that the entire atmosphere and traditions must have seemed bewildering and not a little frightening, especially if the litigant was on trial for his life.

I loved the musty smell of the courts, the apparent courtesy of the advocates and the aura of quiet maturity given off by the judges who wore red robes as they then did in England.

But never will I forget the day I witnessed a man being sentenced to death. I cannot recall for what crime he was thus sentenced but I do recall the judge donning a black piece of cloth atop his cream wig and pronouncing sentence upon a young African who, but a few feet from where I was, stood shaking whilst learning his fate. I don't know whether that sentence was in due course carried out but I have no reason to believe that it wasn't. There was nothing unusual about the passing of a death sentence in that country in those days: it didn't receive major press publicity, save in the rare event that the recipient was white, though I recall no such instance.

There were no juries in trials when the accused was black. In such cases, the judge sat with two assessors whose background was as district commissioners, the judge directing his assessors as to the relevant law and the majority deciding the facts in accordance with those directions. Whites had the benefit of trial by jury. This system was no doubt intended to recognise the fact that an all-white jury (black people were not eligible) was unlikely to be perceived as impartial when a black person was the accused. In cases where the litigants were black, African customary law was applied, but not in the realm of criminal law and not where the custom was 'repugnant to natural justice and morality' (the African Law and Customs Act), which meant, of course, repugnant to Western standards of morality. The test was whether a law so outraged accepted standards of ethics as to create a sense of revulsion. This last snippet I garner from a book by Professor Claire Palley who, as we shall later see, was instrumental in my decision to study law in England.

Strangely perhaps, the common law system was Roman-Dutch law, after the system which prevailed in South Africa, the only other part of the world in which that system obtained being Ceylon, as it then was, now Sri Lanka. But procedurally it was all much the same as in England and Wales. Most of the lawyers secured their law degrees in South Africa, and the profession was divided between attorneys (solicitors) and advocates (barristers) and there was never any question in my mind but that I was going to be an advocate.

Dad was slightly acquainted with the Chief Justice, Sir Hugh Beadle, because (I think) he dabbled in farming in his spare time and came to the farm to buy a beast or two. Beadle was a short man with a moustache and never struck me as naturally born to the high station which he occupied; maybe that's because the only time I saw him he wasn't robed but was at ease in the dust-blown atmosphere of a farm. In the days of Federation (of Rhodesia and Nyasaland) there were also federal courts of which Sir Robert Tredgold was Chief Justice. He later became acting Governor General of the Federation.

I remember the day our 'A' level results were published. Though mine were disappointing, a group of us gathered to while away the rest of the day at the Parkview Club playing snooker. One participant was my classmate whose father had committed suicide and another was a classmate named Barry Tustin.

It is strange that the memory of that day and especially of Barry Tustin has stayed with me so long. Barry and I were not close friends. We had little in common, though he was a pleasant enough colleague and bright, but not part of my circle of close friends. He was killed not long after that day in a motor vehicle accident in Zambia, an event which had a marked effect on me in that I would sometimes think I saw him in the street and I even occasionally dreamt of him. Quite why that had such an effect upon me I have never managed to fathom. Whilst the faces of many of my classmates are now to me a blur, I can still conjure up Barry's face as clearly as he was that pleasant afternoon in the summer after I had finally left school. I wonder what would have become of him had he not taken that fateful car journey. It is perhaps a trite thought – and certainly not an original one – that so many years have passed whilst I have studied and married and had children and grandchildren and laughed and cried and yet all those years he was not alive when, but for a stupid mishap, he would have been.

Chapter Twenty-Two

It is no filial exaggeration to say that Dad was known throughout the farming community of Rhodesia. He was a larger-than-life character, whose knowledge of cattle and breeding them was second to none which was perhaps not surprising given that this had been at the epicentre of his life since he had been a boy. From his small beginning in Figtree in the late 1930s, he eventually became one of the biggest land-owners in the country, with one ranch enclosing some fifty-two miles of dirt road. His ranches tended to bear English place names, including Reigate, Ascot and Ravenswood though the terrain and the views could hardly have been less green and English.

Horses were a side line, as were mules which he imported from South Africa. When my two sons came out to Africa, years after I had left, for their summer holidays he presented them with a horse each. He had named them (the horses, not my sons) Chilimanski and Shmok. Of course, they didn't take the horses back to Hong Kong with them at the close of the holidays but each year they expected to see Chilimanski and Shmok on their summer returns to Rhodesia. This created a problem. Dad didn't keep the horses he acquired. Horses were for purchase and sale and Chilimanksi and Shmok just happened to be two of the horses on Reigate Farm when the boys first visited. They were sold soon after the boys left. So in advance of the subsequent visits, Dad had hurriedly to scour Matabeleland for two mounts that looked as exactly as the two originals as was feasible. The ruse tended to work.

The range of cattle in which Dad and later Henry dealt was wide: Aberdeen-Angus, Africaner, Charolais, Hereford, Friesland, Jersey, Tuli, Sussex, Simmenthal and Brahman and sometimes a mixture. Dad and Henry were one of the first cattlemen in the country to import Brahman bulls from Texas and Henry went to Texas on a learning and buying venture.

The Stocks stocked Brahman and Brangus bulls and very well they did too. The Bulawayo Agricultural Show took place each year at the Trade Fair grounds and more than once did we win the champion bull prize. The biggest prize of all was the 1000 Guinea Gold Trophy for the champion bull of Rhodesia and a bull owned by Henock Ranching named Lazy Three Baron 18 was selected for this signal honour which resulted in a photograph of Dad with President Wrathall on the front page of the Bulawayo Chronicle – the photograph did not include Lazy Three Baron, which I thought a little unfair.

Sales of Henock Brahmans were well advertised and weren't restricted to Rhodesia. There was a sale of them in South Africa with names for the bulls such as Henock Rexcrata Sturgeon and Henock Rexcrata Honolulu and Henock I.W. Minnehaha. The names originated in America but although Henry and Dad knew them by these exotic names, I did not. I saw them from time to time on visits to Reigate Farm but I could barely tell one from the other.

On another occasion we won the prize for champion Brahman bull for a large beast named Tiberius. This time the prize was handed out by one Denis Norman, Minister of Agriculture and the newspaper showed the bull as well as Dad and the minister who, the caption said, was taking a close look at the animal – it seemed to me that Mr Norman was keeping a healthy distance.

I say 'we' won the prizes as in 'we' the family, but the effort and the success was not mine or even partly mine. But still, I took pride in the achievement. My parents had been through dreadful times in their lives; Dad had been beaten up for his ethnicity and Mom had, through murder, lost those dearest to her. Mom and Dad had arrived in this strange country penniless and not speaking any of the languages which were the currency of conversation and yet through sheer hard work and talent, they had achieved much in terms of material and reputational success. It was not a unique achievement for it was symptomatic of the success of many refugees worldwide but it was nonetheless an achievement which was singularly uplifting to contemplate and recognise.

Mules were difficult to come by. They had to be imported from the Cape in South Africa but that in turn required exchange control permission which was not always easy to obtain. Dad used to breed mules using a Catalonian jack donkey and a mare, and some mules were bred using a horse stallion and a donkey mare but the results were small mules; South African mules were better. I have no idea who needed mules or for what purpose though I have read that some were used for ploughing and some by forestry personnel for dragging logs.

Dad was always well-dressed, even when he was out in the bush: jacket and tie and a neat hat, and immaculately polished shoes. The only time he disrespected his hat was the occasion on which a farmer asked a price too high at which Dad threw his hat in the dust of the kraal where the beasts on sale were on view, stamped on the unfortunate headpiece and told the farmer that the ruination of the hat was the farmer's fault since but for the exorbitant asking price, the hat would have stayed on its proper perch. The bewildered farmer dropped his demand, a deal was struck and the hat retrieved and dusted down.

Sales were the preserve, by and large, of the Tunmer family, well known cattle auctioneers in the country. They operated primarily out of Gwelo (now changed to Gweru) and three generations of that family had conducted business with Dad. Of my father one of the Tunmer's once wrote that 'Ernie Stock's superior knowledge of livestock has been recognised not only in Zimbabwe but in many countries outside its borders.'

Attending cattle sales with Dad was an experience not to be forgotten. There was little talk on the way there and little on the way back for he was invariably immersed in his small notebook calculating what he would buy and for how much, how many he had bought, what they would cost to feed and what they would, in due course, fetch.

Once there, he was cheerfully greeted by all and sundry; by his farming friends, by competitors and especially by the auctioneers since his very presence meant an active bidding war.

We would sit at the back row of the buyers' stand, with the benefit of fine sandwiches made by Mom for the trip. Hat askew, with cigarette holder but no cigarette held between his teeth, he would mutter and bid and occasionally disrupt the entire process by offering a bid significantly lower than the immediately preceding one.

After Henry joined him in the business and as his experience grew, Dad would take more of a back seat and let Henry do the bidding. Henry had vision for an even grander scale of ranching and was much instrumental in the development of the Brahman herds but his plans were rendered difficult by the growing political unrest in the country. Dad was an excellent teacher of cattle craft but he was not a light taskmaster and it wasn't always easy for Henry to please him.

I was no farmer and there was never a question of my joining that calling. Indeed, Dad suggested that I knew not the difference between a cow and a bull but that was not quite true. Not quite. I had trouble identifying weaners and heifers but cows and bulls I knew.

Business was conducted from an office in town, an office which was probably the least plush in the city. It occupied a place opposite the Southern Sun Hotel in 10th Avenue and stood shoulder to shoulder with the best steakhouse in the province.

The office housed two old desks, one for Dad, the other for his bookkeeper, Mrs Hale. There were one or two leather armchairs which had seen better days and into which those who intended to pose a tough negotiating stance were sunk into hopelessness.

There was a window display of sorts: saddles and other riding gear and various black and white photographs on the walls inside, of Brahman bulls and of Henry and Dad in their Stetson hats and a notice which amused Dad: 'When in this office, please speak in low dulcet tones for when pushed I am apt to be a most unpleasant bastard.'

Business never ceased. When not on one of the farms or in his office, Dad was at home on the phone, often until late at night, phone calls to farmers were phone calls to remote parts of the country for which it was necessary to book a call through an operator. These were known as trunk calls. So well-known was Dad's voice to the operators, that it became unnecessary for him to identify himself or the number from which he was calling.

Listening to his phone conversations was a pastime in itself. The objective of each call, often after bedtime, was to effect a deal, but the run up to the real business was invariably a prolonged inquiry into the health of the person contacted and his family.

"How are you, Mr Connelly?.. Me too. I've not been well. I went to the doctor and he said … And how is Mrs Connelly? … Mrs Stock is fine … Well, she gives me plenty trouble … But never mind – all that matters is good health … And how are your sons? … Yes, Henry is well … Frankie is studying. He's a bit thin and he's had the flu. But I have a bull for you, a Hereford which in all my years in this country is the best bull I have ever seen … If you're not interested in that one, I have an even better one."

All the while, Mom fussed over him, telling him to stop speaking and did he have nothing else to do but talk over the phone? And why did he not dress more warmly when he went out (for it was only thirty degrees centigrade in the shade)?

And she stood in the kitchen from morn 'til night supervising the cooking, baking butter biscuits and making sure the house was spotlessly clean.

She suffered badly with psoriasis on her scalp and for some reason I could never fathom, this irritated Dad. I suppose it happens to all married couples, that some of their habits irritate and the irritation, once it takes root, grows with the passage of time. Thus it is that I block my ears when my wife crunches an apple; she when I chew on a chicken bone; my father when my mother scratched her scalp and when Henry crunched ice. "Hor doch auf" (Stop it already) he would say to her and she would tell him how fortunate he was not to suffer the same malady and the developing tension would only cease by him going to the study to make another call.

And when Henry crunched ice, Dad would tell him that nice people did not crunch ice, and when I started a meal without first taking some bread and thanking the Lord for the morsel, I was told not to come to the table like a heathen. And if I left the table before grace was said, I was told not to leave the table like a heathen. At least I didn't crunch ice; maybe heathens did.

Chapter Twenty-Three

My parents' acquaintances were an eclectic crowd. They were farming community acquaintances, butchers, doctors, accountants, auctioneers, veterinarians, and members of the Jewish community.

Major George Errington was a farmer who lived out in Figtree. His farm was Monckton Ranch and he had been a recipient of the Military Cross, though he never boasted about that. His wife was the daughter of Major General Sir Henry Augustus Busham and some said that she was a cousin of the queen. Of England. They spoke highly-polished English and were without doubt embedded in the English upper class.

Dad was great friends with and a business colleague of the major. I think that the major purchased beasts from Dad.

Dad's English was never great in that he spoke with an accent which was difficult to place – it didn't sound German to me and he would have hated it so described. But he conversed at ease and occasionally threw in a word or two of German when he spoke with the major, for the major knew some German, no doubt from the time he had been in the British army.

They came from a world apart, did the Erringtons, yet the social mixing with Dad's world was never awkward. They had an abiding respect for each other. The Erringtons dressed immaculately as did Mom and Dad, but were never showy or glitzy. They epitomised English aristocratic understatement and every summer returned to England to re-establish contact with their roots. I think that they had an apartment in London for I recall one year being a guest at a cocktail function at their place in Chelsea – or was it Kensington? – where they introduced me to a cousin or good friend by the name of Lord Gerald Upjohn whom the major said had done rather well.

Rather well indeed, I'd say. Lord Gerald Upjohn was a Law Lord who took a kindly interest in my career and invited me to lunch in the House of Lords when I was a law student. Not only that, it happened, fortuitously, that he presided on Call Night the evening I was called to the Bar at Lincoln's Inn. As is so often the case with those who are at the top of their professional tree, he had no need for airs and graces; he was the embodiment of modesty and refinement.

From a rather different milieu came John Parry. He was no Major Errington. I don't know what his background was but he was a voluble character, large in girth and large in his appetite for whisky. When Boswell's circus came to town he managed to fall under the spell of the snake charmer, a blonde German lady named Elsa, and so into our house from time to time to partake of Mom's excellent cooking and Dad's ever decreasing supply of whisky, came Big John and the charming snake charmer.

As their name suggests, and as their accents attested, the Connelly brothers were Irish. Mom and Dad had met them and their father in Figtree when first they arrived in the country from Germany. The Connelly boys were teenagers at the time and were open mouthed and more than a little amused at meeting these people who spoke not a word of English.

The Connellys were a farming family too and the relationship between Dad and that family was one of great fun and laughter and fondness, and if my information is correct the family is still represented in that neck of Africa though by all accounts they haven't been treated well by the authorities there. They are white and they are farmers, not an auspicious mix in the political climate of that benighted place. Once Mugabe took power, many, perhaps most, farmers, had their farms confiscated without compensation and given to political cronies who soon ran the land and their farming stock into arid, non-productive enterprises, thereby ensuring the ultimate bankruptcy of the country and the abject poverty of the rural African. Farmers whom Dad had known were murdered. It seemed as if the Stock family had a habit of choosing dangerous places to live.

Dad's solicitor was David Stirling of the firm Coghlan and Welsh. Stirling was a quietly-spoken man whose main function in life was to persuade my father not to sue whenever the mood so took him. Which was often. In this sound advice Stirling didn't always succeed and Dad's performances as a litigant and witness were renowned for their absence of muted presentation, but more often than not, he amused the Bench and found himself on the winning side. So threats to 'sue the bastard' were taken seriously and were often sufficient in themselves to achieve their objective.

Roger Hounsell was the family accountant. For many years, from the days when he first qualified to the days after my parents had passed away and Henry and I needed to know the details of this transaction or that going back thirty years perhaps or more, we could count on Roger remembering all the details. And I mean *all* the details. Even ones we didn't require. Most sentences emanating from Roger commenced with the phrase "You remember I told you …" And more often than not we couldn't remember what he had told us and more often than not it was impossible to get a word in edgeways and it was not uncommon to leave a meeting in a stupefied state, gasping for air and asking each other what the outcome had been. But he was a bright man and adept at dealing with companies and problems much more sophisticated than ours, but he was fond of our parents as they were of him, and he remained a loyal advisor and such a fan of Mom's cooking that his meetings with Dad were invariably arranged to coincide with dinner at our place.

Jimmy Gilchrist was the French consul in Bulawayo, though what connection he had with France was a puzzlement for he was as British as they come and one of his trademark features were his bushy upturned eyebrows. I spent some time in my teen years fruitlessly trying to train my eyebrows the Gilchrist way for I thought it would lend me an air of Francophile culture.

Then there was R.T. Little, another Englishman who was noteworthy for many things no doubt, but I found him noteworthy for the lugubrious shape of his eyes. The lower eyelids drooped, like a cocker spaniel's, and I was given to wondering whether beneath the lower lids, there might be a gremlin pulling them ever further downwards. He had a pale pink face and he spoke in a manner sympathetic to the condition of his eyelids which is to say, slowly and ponderously.

Given the nature of Dad's business, there was often the need for a veterinary surgeon to attend to a sick cow or bull or horse, to deliver a calf and to predict when the latest quarantine on account of foot and mouth disease might be lifted. One vet, whose name I think was Lithgow, was a man of diminutive proportions. Quite how he managed to reach a horse's rear end when occasion demanded puzzled me. Perhaps he used a stool.

The city seemed to attract medics of small physical stature. Our recurrent GP (recurrent because the family was given to recurring medical complaints) was Dr Nussbaum who reached 5 foot 3 inches at a stretch and who diverted attention from his size by sporting a healthy moustache. He seemed always in a rush, conferring an air of urgency to his house calls, of which in our case there were many, shooting in and out, with swift but generally accurate diagnoses and a ready smile. By the time we came to pronounce the usual "Thank you, doctor, for coming out so late," he was already out of sight, down the pathway and into his tiny vehicle, deliberately tiny, no doubt, so as to make him appear taller. It was Dr Nussbaum who diagnosed that I had contracted a mild dose of yellow fever from a vaccination provided before our European trip in 1955. Whilst yellow fever was not endemic to Europe of course, it was to the Sudan, I think, where we were scheduled to make a stop. Naturally, my family assumed, when the ailment was diagnosed, that it was likely in my case to be fatal. Dr Nussbaum could count on my father asking at the outset, in the middle, and at the end of any medical examination, even if the cause was a common cold, whether 'it' was serious. That too, I suspected, was driven by superstition, that if one asked, the fatal illness would prove non-fatal.

Of the butchers in town, of whom there was quite a large number, most seemed to be of the Hebrew persuasion. Dad didn't tend to get on well with them, save for the week approaching the Day of Atonement. The rest of the year was given to unbridled rivalry.

First in line was Walter Heilbron, of German Jewish extraction, who owned the Dundee Butchery. Then there was Kurt Gonsenhauser who ran another butchery which was probably called Gonsenhauser Butchery and also a butchery owned by cousin Sam's father, Leiser Leiserowitz, and Leiser's partner, Mr Gilbert. Legend has it that Leiserowitz went with his second wife, Beryl, to Italy and came back reporting to Gilbert that they had, whilst in Italy, been to the opera. Gilbert, though steeped in the entrails of butchered animals, was not steeped in the arts and readily confessed that he didn't know what an opera was. Leiserowitz, with an inimitable ability to calibrate explanations appropriate to his audience, requested his partner to imagine a customer coming into the butchery to ask for a pound of kosher sausages, but to envisage that the request was not delivered in ordinary speech but rather in song. That was opera. And to illustrate the point, Leiserowitz delivered there and then in the shop, first in ordinary unsung speech, the question, "Mr Gilbert, may I please have a pound of kosher sausages?" with the spoken answer, "Certainly, Mr Customer, here is a pound of kosher sausages." That, said Leiserowitz, was not opera. It was ordinary speech. Then the same question and answer were repeated but this time, to a flourishing tune of his own composition, with suitable theatrical hand gestures. That, he explained, with an air of cultured superiority, was opera. Gilbert, suitably impressed and grateful for the demonstration, decided that that was all he needed to know about that art form and never thereafter acquired a taste for Puccini, perhaps believing that it was a variety of mushroom.

Bobbie Frenkel was a wholesale merchant who had his offices and warehouse in Fife Street across the road from our house when we lived in that street. Bobbie had a round and red face with creases about the eyes that suggested he was ever ready for a laugh. Perhaps because their businesses were never destined to cross paths, Dad and Bobbie were buddies and each given to practical jokes on the other. Sometimes this went too far as on the occasion when Dad phoned Bobbie at six one morning to tell him that a large trailer truck wishing to deliver goods had arrived across the road from our house with a delivery for the business but, seeing no-one there, was ready to return to its base in Northern Rhodesia. Frenkel dressed frantically, and broke every speed limit record to drive from his house in Khumalo to prevent this threatened costly breach of contract, only to behold Dad standing outside shaking with laughter, no truck in view, no truck ever having been in view.

Harold Kluk, also Jewish, also with a moustache, was our local chemist; Solly Jossel was an insurance broker; the dentist, Dr Golden, was certainly Jewish; Eric Cohen was the Jewish heart specialist (meaning that he was Jewish and specialised in Jewish hearts); the Silvers were the photographers; the Lobel family baked all the bread and biscuits. All in all, we Jews had the place sewn up. The anti-Semites were correct: we were taking over the world.

The Wolfermans didn't feature on our social radar but I had occasion to rue that fact some years later when Henry and I were lunching at a beach restaurant in Cape Town and a lady at the far end gave us a wave. We assumed, correctly as it transpired, that she must have recognised us, that she hailed from our home town and that we were supposed to know who she was. At the end of her meal, she and her husband came over and, being the gentlemen we undoubtedly were, we stood. Accusingly, she suggested that we didn't recognise her. I silently prayed for swift recall, but to no effect. We lied and said of course we knew who she was. "No, you don't," she perspicaciously remarked, and reminded us that she was from Bulawayo and that her surname was Wolferman. "Of course!" I exclaimed, now so deeply mired in pretence that there was no backing down and I added, since a flash of inspired memory, in belated answer to my earlier prayer, came to me all at once, "Of course I remember you," I said, "I knew your daughter Eve." And I smiled with premature self-congratulation and relief, only to be horror-struck by her response: "But I am Eve."

There were many others whose omission from this tale is not intended in disrespect but the tale must have an ending. Mr Pickard was always pale and ill; Mr Amato was always jovial and teasing Dad, to his considerable amusement, about the archetypal German Jewish refugee given to exaggerating the size of the business empire he had been forced to abandon.

"I had," went his mantra in a faux German accent, "ein factory so big in Chermany, that the office was in Cologne and the toilet in Hamburg."

Barney Gunn merits special mention. He wasn't a social acquaintance but a farm manager in Dad's employ, a thoroughly decent fellow ever eager to please but difficult to address or hear out because of his restless habit of hopping from one foot to the other. It seems that he found it impossible to stand still; so much so that it caused eye strain for his interlocutors whose attempts to keep him in view were akin to watching a tennis ball flowing at speed from one end of a court to the other and back again.

There were, with the passage of time, African colleagues too, one of whom I have previously mentioned, namely, Joshua Nkomo. It wasn't long before we entertained them in our house. This sounds like some grand concession and it may be odd to the outsider that the point is made at all. Yet given the social history of the country, it represented a change in fact and was not in our household viewed as a concession. When it happened, it happened without an air of awkwardness. But it was nonetheless a change and therefore itself a mark of how layered and discriminatory society had long been.

Anti-African sentiments were not part of our conversation, though in truth the prospect of African political advancement was viewed with misgiving for the fear was of political instability and of racial retribution.

With the passage of time, as befalls all communities, these characters grew old and most of my parents' friends eventually made their way to Sixth Avenue extension, which was Dad's name for the Jewish cemetery.

The synagogue burnt down some years later, the result, it was said, of someone cooking his evening meal near a wall of the building and not putting out the embers. The youth of the Jewish community, or most of them, left the country for places where future prospects seemed brighter, so that in due course, the community shrunk to a size almost too small to conjure a prayer forum of ten males.

The Sixth Avenue extension location – the cemetery – is to this day immaculately kept. The gravestone engravings form a record of the life of the Jewish community of that city, of a vibrant era, of friends now no more; housing the resting places of my Uncle Simon who passed away when I was three weeks old; of Uncle Alfred who died when I was recovering from my appendix operation; of his wife Selma, my father's sister; and of my dear parents whose lives have been lived and whose travails, like those of millions others, are denigrated by a bigotry of over two thousand years.

This pot-pourri of Jews, these characters, actors on a remote, dry, dusty, yet sunny stage where opportunity for a decent life was there for the taking, had by and large made the best of their disparate circumstances and lived in a colonial time-warp, preparing their children for a wider world. In that aim at least, they succeeded.

Chapter Twenty-Four

The University College of Rhodesia and Nyasaland (UCRN) has been described by Professor Michael Gelfand as a non-racial island of learning. It certainly was that. It was an island in the sense that it was from the outset the only non-racial educational institution in the country so that those whites – and blacks – who were principled or brave enough to apply to it for entrance to degree courses were in for a culture shock. Their upbringing hitherto had been steeped in the camaraderie of their own ethnicity. Suddenly they were to be thrown together in mixed-race halls of residence, attend lectures with those of other races, eat in the same dining facilities and, more likely than not, socialise with each other outside the confines of their new formal setting.

The university was established by Royal Charter in 1955 and was affiliated to London University. The medical school was established in 1963 and was affiliated to Birmingham University.

The campus was a sprawling affair in that area of Salisbury appropriately known as Mount Pleasant and it comprised several modern halls of residence, teaching blocks and playing fields with a fine view of the city in the relatively near distance.

It was at this institution that I commenced my tertiary education and it was here that I spent my last months living in the country of my birth, months that were serenely happy and exciting, perhaps the freest I have ever experienced.

How did I end up there?

Most white scholars who had completed their 'A' levels went to universities in South Africa. That had for long been the tradition. Cape Town University seemed to be the university of choice. It had a fine international reputation and a magnificent setting. Others, for various reasons, went to Rhodes University in Grahamstown, a few to the University of Natal in Durban and some to Witwatersrand University in Johannesburg.

Law in South Africa could only be studied as a postgraduate degree. Most aspiring to a law degree first aimed for a degree in commerce or one in arts; the LL.B came later. The idea of broadening one's education before narrowing the focus to law was a good one and I duly applied to Cape Town University and was accepted there with College House allotted as the hall of residence where I would first reside.

This allocation was not ideal, for College House had a bad reputation for its fresher inductions which went on for months and were harsh. Of the least harmful pranks related by anecdote was the reassembly of a motor vehicle in a student's upstairs accommodation whilst he was out, topped only by the taking of a horse with diarrhea up the stairs to the room of another student.

But it was not the induction terrors that persuaded me to try elsewhere.

The future did not lie in a degree from South Africa, a milieu steeped in racial disharmony and discrimination, even though the universities there were hotbeds of resistance to the apartheid regime and its laws. An English qualification was a better insurance against the vagaries of Africa as it was then developing and an education in English law and some practice at the English Bar was an education and experience at the heart of the common law world. Whatever the future was to hold, this was a sensible move.

In 1964, there was no law faculty at the university in Salisbury and it was decided that I would forward applications to universities in the UK to study law there but would start a degree course at UCRN whilst I awaited the outcome of those applications. The year at UCRN commenced in January whilst the academic year at English universities started in September or October.

I opted for the B.Sc. (Economics) degree course, though why, I cannot recall, since economics bored me. Nevertheless the course took in other subjects of greater interest including social anthropology and law.

I applied to and was accepted by UCRN. I was allotted to the Manfred Hodson hall of residence.

I took the overnight train from Bulawayo to Salisbury and arrived with a certain degree of awe and lightheartedness at the campus, armed with toothbrush and toothpaste, probably a tomato sandwich or two packed by Mom, and an abundance of suitably casual clothing.

I settled in quickly and there were one or two of my former classmates from Milton High but very few. The racial mix was white, black and Indian. My room in Hall was convenient and relatively spacious, one or two floors up with a wide window overlooking the dining hall and the campus.

I soon befriended Paul Liptz. Paul became my closest friend. He was a Salisbury lad, ginger-haired, bespectacled and with a mischievous air. He was there to study history, a subject which he took so much to heart that in due course he pursued his interest as an academic in Israel to which country he moved in 1967 when the Six Day War erupted.

There were few things that didn't send Paul and me into convulsions; from the time he woke me at two in the morning, knocking urgently on my door saying, when I asked why, that he merely wanted to check whether I was awake, to his insane delight at my propensity to trip over uneven ground. This propensity has stayed with me for the subsequent fifty years or so. Put a pebble in my path and my foot will find it and stumble. I flew thousands of miles in the summer of 2018 to attend a colleague's surprise 80th birthday party in Provence. Months of planning had been devoted to the surprise, the denouement of which was that about thirty colleagues from different corners of the globe were to hide behind a hedge in the chateau grounds as the octogenarian was, at an agreed time, taken by his devoted wife from indoors to the gardens when we were, at a given signal, all to rise and serenade the birthday boy with a hearty rendition of Happy Birthday. The time duly was upon us and we maintained complete silence upon and after arrival at the chateau. Eventually, we sensed the presence of the birthday boy and his attentive wife. We crouched and edged ourselves closer to the hedge to ensure we were not seen, ready excitedly for the signal. As we all moved closer to the edge of the hedge (no poetry intended) to make absolutely sure we were not seen, I stumbled on an uneven paving stone and fell through the hedge into the birthday boy's arms, badly twisting my ankle in the process. It was a surprise indeed, though not quite according to the script. Paul didn't witness this debacle but I am sure he would have wished to for it was just one in a long line of tripping mishaps.

He and I were given to outbursts of mirth so readily, for reasons that by any objective analysis were not funny at all, that we were often helpless with laughter, to the extent of hindering the passage of students up or down staircases because we were collapsed in pain in their path.

Rag Week was not without its challenges. A hallmark of the week was steeped in the tradition of a battle between the students of the university and those attending Gwebi Agricultural College some distance out of town. The object of the exercise was to see who first would capture the Rag Queen of the other's institution. To do so would involve skirmishes along the way to the objective. And the skirmishes could get nasty. Capturing a male rival was commonplace as was the shaving of his head, the denuding of the captive and abandoning him on a country road with nothing but a leaf to cover his delicate parts whilst he attempted, with little hope of success, to hitch a ride back into town.

The week had challenges of another kind, when we roamed the streets of Salisbury in costumes whilst artistic floats went on parade and we tried to sell copies of the students' magazine to unwilling motorists whom we approached at traffic lights.

That was when the antipathy of some whites to the fact of a multi- racial institution in their midst first revealed itself to me. A few gave willingly enough to our charity but quite a few did not, and announced their reason with forceful denunciations of our supposed communist affiliations. If we were prepared to mix socially and educationally with blacks, we must be communists. That was the refrain of some, both in Rhodesia and in South Africa, in answer to attempts to encroach upon racial barriers.

That the university was a hotbed of political dissent cannot be denied and it should have come as no surprise to any thinking person. Here were black students who had climbed the educational ladder despite economic and other obstacles and yet their very skin colour was likely of itself to spell a hindrance to advancement in the society into which history had placed them. Small wonder then that they were sore and were prepared to stick out their necks.

It follows that student debates were fiery events, by comparison with which I was later to find student debates in England tame and student anger contrived.

One of the main protagonists was a white student named Judith Todd, the daughter of Sir Garfield Todd who had been prime minister of Rhodesia, both of whom were in due course to find themselves detained in prison by the Smith Government, as was Shakespeare Makoni whose name was difficult to forget so unShakespearean was he in looks and bluntness of discourse.

Paul and I made friends with a group of Indian students with whom we somehow felt an affinity the cause of which was difficult to identify. Perhaps it was because they too, like the Jews, were a minority, but with similar cultural family and work values. For the first time in my life, I was invited to the homes of Indian families where we were spoiled with outstanding and hot Indian cuisine.

Social anthropology was a subject quintessentially suited to Africa given its plethora of tribes and tribal customs, of which the whites, with the possible exception of farmers, were largely ignorant. We studied the social habits of the Nuer whose dwelling place was Sudan, some works by the famous anthropologist, Professor Evans-Pritchard, and African belief in the power of witchcraft.

The hold which witchcraft exercised over many indigenous Africans was not news to me. Few white employers had not encountered it amongst their African employees – the preference for the remedies of witchdoctors and the belief in it as a cause of personal or family misfortune. A common approach to a mishap was to recognise the immediate visible cause, such as a vehicle striking a pedestrian, but the answer to what caused the vehicle to strike lay in witchcraft.

Truth to tell, the whites held this to be nonsense, ignorant mumbo jumbo, but there was always a hint of 'what if there's something in it,' a thought which we were never inclined to admit.

Many years later, I was told a haunting story by a white South African doctor – I will call him James – a highly sophisticated man in his fifties at the time of the event in question. He was something of an expert in the field of African wildlife and spent such vacation time as he could muster in the bush, finding game to watch or merely absorbing the beauty of the African veld and the vast star-bedecked skies at night.

One of his white medical colleagues – whom I will call Steve – was not only well versed in the traditions of witchcraft but purported to practice it too, though not in the course of his medical practice and never to effect mischief.

Steve emigrated to California where he established a reputation as an excellent physician but every year he returned to South Africa and spent time with James in the bush.

On the occasion I wish to describe, it was the penultimate evening of such a sojourn and the two men were replete, having eaten their dinner round the campfire. Steve told James that he wished to throw bones, with James as the subject of the inquiry to be constituted by the exercise. James pooh-poohed the idea, telling Steve that whilst he respected him and his interest in witchcraft, he could not bring himself to treat the process seriously and feared that he might by his cynicism spoil what had been an excellent week's friendship. Steve asked James to humour him nonetheless and the bones were thrown. Steve studied them and rapidly expressed alarm. Despite no hint of any illness in James, Steve insisted that it was imperative for the two to leave the remote area at once and speed to a hospital in Johannesburg. James scoffed at the notion and insisted on turning in for the night. Whilst asleep he dreamt for the first time in years of his deceased mother who, in the dream, expressed grave concern for him. So disturbed was he by the strangeness of the dream and by what had gone before that he agreed to cut the holiday short and return to Johannesburg and seek an early health check.

They left, James was subjected to a medical check and within 24 hours underwent triple by-pass surgery but for which, he was later advised, he would have died. He is now a fitness fanatic who engages in arduous cycling tours of such ferocity that I fear for his health, witchcraft or no witchcraft.

The reader's reaction to this story is likely to be one of disbelief but I know James too well to doubt for one moment the veracity of his account.

My academic mentor at UCRN was Professor Claire Palley, a most interesting lady who in due course became Principal of St Anne's College, Oxford. Her subject was law and I was sufficiently taken with the course she delivered to come top of the class in the mid-year exams. Her husband was Dr Arn Palley, who was both a medical doctor and a lawyer and the only independent member of the Rhodesian Parliament of the day.

Professor Palley knew of my desire to study law and be called to the Bar and she encouraged me to apply to universities in the UK.

This I did. My 'A' level results had not been good enough to have any chance of securing a place at either Oxford or Cambridge which to this day I regret, though I have derived vicarious pleasure from the fact that both my sons studied at Oxford and one at Cambridge too.

I eventually aimed for the law faculty of Liverpool University, a faculty of solid though not top rank reputation. I am forced to confess that one of the motivating factors for this choice was my friendship with a young lady I met that year who was visiting Rhodesia and was then a student at that university. Her name was Mary somebody or other and she spoke well of it. I knew no one in England save the Golding family who lived in London. The notion of leaving the country of my birth for several years, a country in which I had enjoyed so much happiness, for what was after all a strange place for me, in times when traveling home for university vacations was not on the cards, was somewhat daunting and the fact of an established friendship at the university to which I would be heading carried a significance which was almost certainly misplaced.

And so I applied for a place at Liverpool University and was accepted for the academic year commencing that October.

But that was months away and in the meantime life in Salisbury was a merry-go-round of some work and lots of play.

I was of course introduced to Paul's family. His father had by then passed away but his mother and his elder brother Cedric lived in an apartment to which I was regularly invited for meals. This was an experience which Cedric particularly enjoyed. His function was to make me uncomfortable by attacking, sotto voce, my table manners.

Being a new visitor to a household is seldom an entirely stress-free experience, especially when one is a youngster amongst adults. On my first visit to the Liptz household, I was, as my parents had trained me to be, on my best behaviour. It was therefore with some discomfort that my ears picked up Cedric's mutter at my first lunch there, evidently directed at me. "He eats like a pig." Paul thought this merited concurrence. "Slurps like a pig too." Mrs Liptz was too concerned that we had an ample sufficiency to notice. "Next, he'll lick his plate," added Cedric, "but what else can one expect? He's from Bulawayo."

The food at Manfred Hodson Hall was not the best. Stew seemed to be the staple diet, either because of a study which had, perhaps, decided that brain cells were thereby enhanced or because the chef's father had hoarded the country's stew in anticipation of a political upheaval that had been threatened but had not materialised.

Eventually, we had had enough. Our complaints, delivered in suitably moderate vein, bore no fruit. No fruit but loads of stew.

So we decided upon a curative ruse which was to place an advertisement in the Salisbury Herald, ostensibly by the university itself which had, according to the advert, mysteriously come by a spare ton of beef of which it wished to dispose on advantageous terms. The ruse worked in the sense that there was a sufficient number of entrepreneurs anxious to make a quick killing with this weighty product of cattle slaughter to result in several telephone calls to the university that day, offering to purchase the surplus meat. Fervent denials that beef was a product in which the University dealt were at first disbelieved but eventually the clamour faded, the culprits not identified and at Manfred Hodson Hall, the stew, like Ol' Man River, kept rolling along.

All the while and as a backdrop to our fun, the winds of change were moving the aims of African nationalism towards their goal of one man, one vote and therefore majority African rule, the end of white rule and independence from colonial rule. Progress to this end was more advanced in Northern Rhodesia and Nyasaland than in Southern Rhodesia where the Rhodesian Front was in government, determined to put off majority rule in that country. In 1963, the British government announced that the Federation was to be dissolved and thereafter began the push by the Rhodesian Front for independence, a push which was not only resisted by the government of the United Kingdom but was concomitant with expressions from that quarter in favour of majority rule. The culmination of this dispute was the Unilateral Declaration of Independence in November 1965.

Whilst these events meant that Dad became more glued to the radio news day by day, certain that every development was a disastrous portent for the survival of his achievements and the well-being of his family, and whilst the political cauldron created steam for the university's student activists and rendered debates exciting and passionate, our daily life was otherwise little affected.

As winter passed that year, I returned to Bulawayo to prepare for my journey to a fresh and uncertain chapter of my life. Leaving Salisbury was painful for I had been blissfully happy there and as I wandered the campus one evening, I paused to look at the university buildings and the city and the African horizon and I knew, as everyone who has lived in Africa knows, that the continent was in my blood, that it would never leave me. And so it has proved.

Chapter Twenty-Five

Bulawayo airport has never been in the running for an airport-of-the-world award. Nowhere is one likely to see Schiphol, Zurich, Hong Kong, Singapore, and Narita bracketed with Bulawayo. It is a small airport building, now as then, the length of an aircraft or two, set about seven miles from town, surrounded by farmland and thorn trees. The same single building houses the facilities for international as well as domestic flights with the same door to the airport apron catering for both. Downstairs is the check-in counter, the currency declaration booth, the passport booth, and the departure lounge which is not really a lounge but a sectioned off area with a few seats looking out onto the apron on which one might, if lucky, see one aircraft but certainly never two. Upstairs houses the relatively basic restaurant, a toilet or two and the outdoor viewing balcony for relatives and friends gathered to greet or to say farewell to those they have come to meet or those they have just dropped off.

Occasionally frantic gestures from the viewing balcony are misinterpreted as exaggerated farewells whereas, as in Harold's case, it is a father trying to tell his embarking son who drove the family vehicle to the airport that he is boarding the plane with his father's car keys in his pocket.

Mom cried of course as I left and Dad could not hide moist eyes, for ours was a close family and Mom especially had centred her life on her husband and sons and would be lonely. I asked them not to be upset and Dad's response lives with me still, "How can I not be upset? You are my son."

Henry wasn't there. He was on a trip in Europe, sowing oats, I think, but not of the kind that had been planted on Reigate Farm. He was due to meet me in London and see me onto the train to Liverpool.

There were no lions on the runway, a hazard that occasionally delayed landing at airstrips elsewhere in the country, such as, within my own experience, at the Victoria Falls.

I flew the one hour it took to reach Salisbury and spent the day with my cousin Greta who, smoking one cigarette after another, provided a meal with applesauce because she knew of my predilection for applesauce with most foods and then she drove me to Salisbury airport which was larger than Bulawayo airport and housed a few more aircraft landed from other centres in Africa and a few from further afield.

Greta shed a tear too; it was in our DNA to shed tears and since she was the oldest in our line of first cousins and I the youngest, there was a bond between us, though the logic of that remark escapes me as much as it will the reader.

The flight to London was an evening flight.

Sat next to me on board was a classmate, Michael Salmon. After my buddy Nehemiah Golub (later Neil Corbett) left the country, Michael always came top of the class. He was good at tennis too. I could forgive him coming top of the class and I could forgive his skill at tennis but I found it difficult to forgive both talents within the same frame.

Michael was a tall individual with a slow and considered method of speech. Quite cool, I suppose.

But as the aircraft lifted off, he was decidedly not cool. He was perspiring noticeably. I wondered whether he was claustrophobic, a prospect that did not appeal for I was not in the mood for a panicky fellow traveler.

I need not have worried. It was not claustrophobia. It was just that he was overweight. Not personally; far from it. It was his luggage that would have been overweight which suggested to him an unusual solution which was to wear two of everything: two sets of underwear, two pairs of socks, two pullovers, and two jackets. I think there was only one pair of shoes.

So it was that I commenced my journey to another land, another continent, another stage of life.

Far below lay Africa, the jacaranda, the thorn trees, the baobabs, the dust, the smell of rain, the disappearing sunset, the vast skies, the lion and the elephant, the cattle in their kraals, the peoples vying for an uncertain future, my friends, my parents and my home.

Bulawayo grew ever more distant as we flew towards the Zambezi River and I sensed that I was crossing a border of a different kind, the one that separates boyhood from a greater maturity, towards increasing personal independence. And I wondered what the future had in store.

But that is another story.